WILL THE MIDDLE EAST GO WEST?

BOOKS BY FREDA UTLEY

LANCASHIRE AND THE FAR EAST

JAPAN'S FEET OF CLAY

JAPAN'S GAMBLE IN CHINA

CHINA AT WAR

THE DREAM WE LOST

LAST CHANCE IN CHINA

LOST ILLUSION

THE HIGH COST OF VENGEANCE

THE CHINA STORY

WILL THE MIDDLE EAST GO WEST?

BY FREDA UTLEY

HENRY REGNERY COMPANY
CHICAGO 1957

LIBRARY OF CONGRESS CARD NUMBER 57-13297

MANUFACTURED IN THE UNITED STATES OF AMERICA

First printing October, 1957
Second printing December, 1957

To my friend Charles E. Lee,
whose encouragement and help were invaluable
in the writing of this book

CONTENTS

PREFACE

I VISITED THE MIDDLE EAST for the first time in December 1956, on the last lap of a seven-months tour of the Far East, Southeast Asia and India. I therefore cannot claim any such expert knowledge of the Middle East as I have gained of the Far East during three decades of study and writing on that area. But the problems of the Arab world today, and the challenge they present to Western statesmanship, are so similar to those we failed to meet in China that I have felt impelled to write this book.

My journey itself, symbolizing as it did a shift in the locus of world crisis, drew my attention from the Far to the Middle East. I was in Formosa when Nasser nationalized the Suez Canal; in Japan and Korea, Hong Kong, Vietnam and Singapore in August and September; in Thailand and Burma during the first half of October; and in New Delhi when Britain, France and Israel launched their attack on Egypt and while Soviet Russia was drowning the Hungarian people's revolution in blood.

After six weeks in India, I spent two weeks in Pakistan and Iran before flying to Lebanon, Jordan and Egypt. In Asia I witnessed at first hand the reactions of friends, enemies and neutrals to America's principled stand on the Suez crisis and, in sharp contrast, their reaction to Pandit Nehru's failure even to speak out unequivocally against Soviet imperialism in Hungary.

Noting and chronicling these reactions, I had no doubt that Vice-President Nixon was right when he said, "history will give eternal credit to our President and the Secretary of State for choosing the hard road of principle." Nor could I doubt, even without waiting for history to pronounce judgment, that Eisenhower's politically courageous and principled stand on Suez had won millions of friends for America in Asia and Africa. Indeed, I had high hopes that the President's action marked the initiation of a policy that would turn the tide in our favor against the Moscow-Peking axis in the East, both Far and Near.

The effect in India was electrical. The leading newspapers, normally subservient to Nehru and therefore anti-American, changed their tune. Nehru was criticized for his failure to utter any outright condemnation of Russia's bloody suppression of the Hungarian people's revolution, while the United States was warmly praised for protecting Egypt against America's closest allies. The old argument which has kept even Nehru's critics quiet—namely, that Soviet Russia checks and restrains "Western imperialism"—no longer seemed to justify Nehru's friendliness toward Moscow and Peking, now that the greatest power in the West was stopping Anglo-French-Israeli aggression against Egypt.

In Pakistan hopes were aroused that America might take a similar principled stand on Kashmir. And when I came to the Middle East, where I spent the month of December, it was wonderful to be able to say, "I am an American," at a moment when decades of distrust of the West among the Arab peoples were being dissipated by evidence that the United States stands for justice and freedom from aggression for all men, irrespective of nation, race or creed.

There was no doubt that America's prestige and influence had been enhanced in Asia and Africa, and even in most European countries; for it is a grave mistake to assume that France and England alone count in the formation of "European" opinion. West Germany, Italy, Greece and Spain welcomed Eisenhower's stand on Suez. The Scandinavian countries, to judge from the conversations I had with Swedish and Danish journalists and officers in Cairo and in the bomb-devastated city of Port Said, were on our side. Canada had stood with us in the United Nations, and even in England we perhaps made more friends than enemies, for many Englishmen opposed Eden's rash, stupid and unprincipled attack on Egypt.

Yet, following my flight back to the United States at the year's end, I was appalled, if not surprised, to find that most American newspapers, columnists and commentators appeared not to know the score. Toward the realities of the dangerous situation in the Middle East they were displaying the same sort of ignorance, indifference or prejudice that most of them had formerly shown concerning China, when they believed that the Communists there were liberal "agrarian reformers."

In India I had been outraged at Nehru's reluctance to take a stand against Russia's attack on Hungary. In America I was shocked to find that many of my former friends and associates, beside whom I have long fought the good fight against the worldwide threat of Communist imperialism, were as myopic in one eye as Nehru in the other.

Yesterday, "liberals" paved the way for the Communist conquest of China, either by their ignorance or their sneaking sympathy for Moscow's Chinese puppets. Today, conservatives and old guard Republicans have taken the lead in advocating a policy on the Middle East as misconceived and misinformed as the policy of President Truman, General Marshall and Dean Acheson on China.

The overwhelming vote given to President Eisenhower last

November shows that the American people have more sense than either liberal or conservative Eggheads. But when the magazines and newspapers of the United States fail to present both sides fully and fairly, the good sense of the American public cannot exert itself against the powerful propaganda of interested foreign pressure groups and their American supporters.

Yesterday, in the case of China, lack of knowledge of the facts, and the powerful influence of the Chinese Communist lobby and its dupes in Washington and the American press, caused our failure to support the Chinese Nationalist Government in its desperate struggle against the Chinese Communist forces armed by Moscow and under her orders. Today, there is a clear and present danger that we shall also unwittingly help the Communists to power in the Middle East—thanks to even more powerful lobbies and to our lack of understanding of the situation, and because the Communists are adept at playing both sides of the street in order to divide and rule. As Mr. Nixon said on May 23, 1957, on his return from his African tour, the Soviet Union and Communist China regard Africa and the Middle East today "as important a target as China was to them 20 years ago—if they can win a substantial number of the uncommitted nations to their Communist side they will gain the balance of power and people and resources in the world which will enable them to bring the free nations to their knees without the necessity of fighting a war."

The problem is how to prevent their doing so. It cannot be done by armaments and economic aid alone. Vital as these are for the defense of the free world, neither can win friends and influence people who have been lost or alienated by political injury. But Communism can be stopped by adherence to American principles which require that we seek to do justice to all and bear malice to none. In seeking to formulate a policy consonant with our traditions and ideals we must however beware both of "reactionaries" who cannot or will not see the underdog's point of view; and of "liberals" who are often confused as to which dog is which.

I do not presume to know all the answers, or to make any but tentative suggestions as to what American policy should be toward the Middle East, with its tangled legacy of broken pledges, old wrongs, injustices, fears, resentment and distrust. I can only hope that the background information which this book supplies may help to build a wise United States policy, serving the interests of both America and the free world, as well as of those aspiring to be free.

FREDA UTLEY

Washington, D. C.
July 1957

WILL THE MIDDLE EAST GO WEST?

I

THE ARAB-CHINA PARALLEL

IN 1923 SUN YAT SEN turned to Soviet Russia for help in the liberation and unification of China, because the Western Powers and Japan refused to relinquish the imperialist privileges and powers which kept China impotent, divided and desperately poor. Thus he unwittingly opened the door to Communist infiltration, subversion and armed attack which a quarter of a century later delivered China over to Communist slavery and converted her into Moscow's most subservient and powerful satellite.

Today, the Arab world is in danger of following the same road to perdition. Once again the West is denying the legitimate national aspirations of a people with an ancient civilization—fallen behind in the march of technological, economic and political progress, and humiliated by past or present subjection to alien rule; but proud of their cultural heritage, longing for strength through unity and progress through reform, and seeking to free themselves from their colonial status, or from fear of renewed aggression and subjugation. In the Arab world, as in China three decades ago, the Western Powers have pursued policies calculated to impel the leaders of the people to call upon Moscow to redress the balance in their favor against old and new imperialisms which seek to retain, regain or win privileges and powers.

Thanks to America's stand on Suez, the disastrous consequences to the Arabs and to the West of any such reliance on the Soviet Power have been at least temporarily averted. But since France and Israel, and to a lesser extent Britain, are today exerting their powerful influence on American opinion to prevent the United States Administration from pursuing an enlightened policy, the danger is by no means past.

History never repeats itself so exactly that its lessons are clear for all to read. Each drama in the continuing record of the "crimes, follies and cruelties" of mankind differs slightly, as the scene shifts, new actors play the leading roles, and the sympathies and judgment of the audience respond to personal and national prejudices, passions, interests and experience. Hence the truth of the cynical observation that the only lesson which history teaches is that mankind learns nothing from it.

Yet there is so close a similarity between the situation in the Arab world today and that of China yesterday that if the West is able to perceive the parallel, we may avoid repeating the errors of judgment and policy which only a few years ago lost almost half a continent to the Communists.

The tragic drama of modern China was long drawn out, and there were times when, as today in the Middle East, temporary periods of enlightened Western statesmanship promised a happier ending. The prologue to the tragedy, played out from 1920 to 1949, when she finally succumbed to the Communists, was similar to that of the Arab drama we are now witnessing, in which America and Russia are both vying for the role of the *deus ex machina.*

In the case of both Chinese and Arabs aggressive Western imperialism in the nineteenth and twentieth centuries followed centuries of subjection to Asiatic conquerors who had caused economic decline and sapped the spirit of the people without destroying their ancient culture and pride of race. In both cases, resentment and suspicion of the West, even after freedom or partial freedom had been won, remained to produce extreme sensitivity concerning human dignity and rights. But, in both, the reaction to the impact of the West was positive as well as negative, since it opened wider horizons and the desire to progress into the modern world through reform or revolution.

China, conquered by the Manchus in the seventeenth century, was still ruled by their degenerate and feeble dynasty in Peking during the nineteenth century, when the Great Powers gradually converted her into what Sun Yat Sen called a "sub-colony" —meaning that while all the Great Powers enjoyed extra-territorial rights and other privileges on China's soil, none of them was obligated to defend her.

Beginning with the First Opium War in 1839, first England and France, then Russia, then Germany and Japan almost tore China to pieces. Territory was seized from her. Colonial areas called "concessions" were established on Chinese soil at Shanghai and in other so-called Treaty Ports. China had to agree to foreigners being exempted from Chinese law and from Chinese taxation (extra-territoriality). Foreign gunboats had the freedom of her rivers and her coasts. Foreign soldiers guarded their nationals even in the capital city of Peking. Foreigners controlled her customs in order to collect the interest due on money borrowed from abroad to pay the "indemnities" imposed on her for being militarily too weak to resist aggression. Increase of tariffs by her government, to protect industries or increase revenues, was forbidden. The ports occupied by the Powers as "leased territory," together with the land close to the railroads which were constructed in the second half of the century, became foreign territory from which China could be attacked if she resisted any demands made on her, and from which the Powers could make war upon one another on Chinese soil. Each concession wrested from her by one Power was at once demanded by the others. The United States, although refraining from armed aggression, insisted under the "most favored nation" clause of her treaties with China that all privileges obtained by others should also be enjoyed by Americans.

Russia, like the United States, did not attack China directly. Instead she acquired huge sparsely inhabited Chinese territories to the north by posing as China's friend. Anticipating the policy of the Soviets, the Czar in 1858 came forward as China's protector, and as his reward for acting as mediator between the Manchu Emperor and the Western Powers, which had already twice defeated China, obtained formal possession from the Chinese Emperor not only of the territories north of the Amur but also of the seacoast as far as Korea and inland to the Ussuri River. At the end of the century the building of the Trans-Siberian railway freed Russia from the domination of British sea power and made her the only Great Power able to exert military pressure directly on China. In 1894 a formal Russo-Chinese treaty of allegiance gave Russia the right to use all Chinese ports in time of war, and soon thereafter she acquired a "lease" of Port Arthur—all, of course, ostensibly for China's "protection."

When the Chinese people in the Boxer Rebellion of 1900 revolted blindly against the intolerable poverty and misery of their existence, they were suppressed by the armed forces of all the Great Powers, in a joint action which culminated in the sack of Peking by British, French, German, Russian and American troops. In the settlement that followed, the Powers signed the 1901 "Boxer Protocol" which established international control over China. In the minds of Britain and the United States, however, the Protocol was not sufficient protection against the threat of Russian domination of China; and the two English-speaking Powers proceeded to build up Japan and subsequently back her in the Russo-Japanese War. Further to prevent the exclusive exploitation of China by any one Power, the United States with British support obtained general agreement on the "Open Door" policy—which, though it later served as the basis for American protection of China against Japan, was basically designed to guarantee the Great Powers freedom of commercial competition in the whole of China.

Thus, before the outbreak of World War I, China was tied hand and foot by the Powers and prevented either from thrusting them out or from building herself up into a strong State. While the rivalries of the Great Powers had kept her from being divided up among them into colonies or protectorates, she had become in effect an international semi- or sub-colony of them all.

The Arab world, about which so much less is known in America than about China, had similar experiences leading to much the same results. The Arabs, like the Chinese, were conquered by Mongol hordes in the thirteenth century; but while Kublai Khan fostered and re-invigorated China's ancient civilization, the Mongols all but destroyed the economic life and flourishing Arab culture of the lands they occupied—notably Mesopotamia (now known as Iraq), where civilization had begun in Babylon thousands of years before and which was then the heart of the Arab world. Egypt and Syria, which then comprised Lebanon and Palestine, escaped the Mongol devastations, but three centuries later came under the dominion of the Ottoman Turks together with Iraq, during the same era which saw the Manchu conquest of China. And in the nineteenth and early twentieth centuries the Turkish sultans in Constantinople, like the Manchu dynasty in Peking, were unable to defend the people they had subjected from the Western imperialist onslaught. England established her dominion over Egypt, and France hers over Morocco and Algeria, during the same century that China was being converted into a "sub-colony" of the Western Powers.

And when, during World War I, the Arabs of the Fertile Crescent won their liberation from Turkey by fighting for England and France, they found they had merely exchanged Turkish for British or French overlords in Iraq, Palestine, Jordan, Syria and Lebanon.

The Arabian Peninsula, consisting largely of desert inhabited by Bedouins, remained independent except for some small British enclaves such as Aden. But the Arab lands under Turkish rule came under British or French direct, or indirect, domination before or after World War I. In China, the Westerners had acquired special privileges and powers extorted by force from the powerless Manchu Government in Peking. In the Middle East and North Africa, Britain and France either ruled through puppet sultans and kings, or, as in the case of Egypt, prior to the 1914 war, were well content to let the Turks incur the unpopularity of the maintenance of their Empire, while the British and French themselves were insulated by their extra-territorial rights and privileges from the disadvantages of corrupt and oppressive Ottoman rule.

The 1914 war constituted a turning point. Up to then, contact with the West, although it meant exploitation and subjection, also had the beneficial result of rousing China and the Arab world from the torpor of centuries. Acquaintance with Western science and techniques awakened them to the need for change and progress in order to defend themselves. Knowledge of Western political ideas and institutions stimulated the desire for liberty. National movements were born in reaction to the humiliation of defeat and subjection to the Western Powers, but at the same time were inspired by Western ideas and principles.

World War I was the great opportunity missed by the West to bring China and the Arab world into our orbit by enabling their peoples to progress under Western influence but free from Western domination.

In both China and the Arab world Wilson's Fourteen Points caused among the intellectual and political leaders of the nationalist movements an upsurge of hope and faith in Western ideals and aims; and the reaction which followed their non-observance at the Paris Peace Conference created similar resentment and disillusionment. In China, the failure of the West to follow its own stated ideals led to the alliance between the Kuomintang and Soviet Russia which was cemented in 1923. In the Arab world it left a legacy of distrust of all Western professions and promises, the result of which, and of the subsequent injuries inflicted upon the Arabs by Britain, France and the United States, are only now fully apparent.

The Arabs during and after World War I were given far greater and more specific cause than the Chinese to distrust western promises. They had entered the war only after receiving written pledges from England that by fighting on her side they would win freedom and independence for the Arab world within its historic boundaries. Their concerted revolt against Turkey in June 1916 came at a time when, thanks to Churchill's ill-fated Dardanelles adventure and the victories of the Central Powers in Europe, British and French fortunes were at their lowest ebb.

The Arab entry into the war, without which Turkey and her German allies might not have been defeated, had been preceded by lengthy negotiations starting in October 1914 when Lord Kitchener, as Minister for War, sent a message on October 31, 1914, to Shareef Husein of Mecca pledging British support to the Arabs in their struggle for freedom if they would enter the war on Britain's side. At first England had tried not to commit herself to any specific pledges. Finally in 1916, on account of hed desperate need of Arab aid, she had agreed to the terms set forth in a document known as the Damascus Protocol which was formulated in July 1915 by leading representatives of the Arab countries assembled in the Syrian capital. These terms included:

(1) The recognition by Great Britain of the independence of the Arab countries in Asia, with the exception of the British colony of Aden.

(2) The abolition of all exceptional privileges granted to foreigners under the "capitulations" (similar to the "extra-territorial" rights in China).

(3) The conclusion of a defensive alliance between Great Britain and the future independent Arab States, along with the grant of economic preferences to Britain.

These terms had been submitted to Britain by the Shareef Husein, who as a descendant of the Prophet and as Keeper of the Holy Cities of Mecca and Medina in the Hejaz, over which he ruled, had great influence in the whole Moslem world, in addition to his prestige as the spokesman of the Arabs whose alliance was sought by Britain. The Arab demands are clearly set forth in Husein's correspondence with Sir Henry MacMahon, who as British Commissioner in Egypt negotiated for the British Government. At first, as the letters which passed between them reveal, MacMahon attempted to leave the Arabs with far less than they wished; but when it became clear that nothing less than the provisions of the Damascus Protocol would induce the Arabs to take the risks and endure the sacrifices which a revolt against Turkey entailed, MacMahon gave the pledges required.

Britain, in agreeing to the main demands of the Arabs through her High Commissioner in Egypt, exempted from the terms of the Damascus Protocol certain small areas deemed not purely Arab—Mersina, Alexandrietta and "portions of Syria lying to the west of the districts of Damascus, Homs, Hama and Aleppo"; and she also insisted that the agreement should not be detrimental to French interests. Otherwise, the British Government unequivocally pledged itself "to recognize and support the independence of the Arabs in all the regions within the limits demanded by the Shareef of Mecca."

Admittedly, by the reservation concerning French interests, the MacMahon correspondence with Husein left the fate of some areas of the Arab world undetermined; but, by any interpretation of the correspondence, the French could claim at most only the northern portions of Lebanon—certainly not all Syria, which they took by force in 1919.

Anyone who reads the documents can have no doubt that the alliance of the Arabs with Britain was clearly based on her acceptance of the Arab demand for freedom and independence within the historic boundaries of the Arab world, extending from the borders of Persia to the Mediterranean and the Red Sea.

The Arabs made a substantial contribution to British victory both militarily and politically. The Arab revolt proclaimed by Husein frustrated a projected German-Turkish expedition to southern Arabia to outflank Aden and block the Red Sea and the Suez Canal to British shipping. The Arabs also contributed no small share to Britain's victory when during General Allenby's campaign in Palestine the Emir Feisal, third son of Husein, commanding a mixed force of Syrian, Palestinian and Iraqi Arabs fighting east of Jordan, defeated as large an army of Turks as the British were facing on the west side of the river and subsequently liberated Damascus. Southwards, under another of Husein's sons, the Arabs held another large Turkish force in check. The Arab revolt not only barred the road to the Red Sea and the Indian Ocean and prevented the Turks from reinforcing their forces in the Dardanelles, it also released British troops from the defense of Egypt and led the Egyptians as members of the Arab community to support Britain's war.

In the words of the American writer, Speiser, in his book *The United States and the Middle East,* "Unquestionably, the British campaign in the Near East owed much of its ultimate success to Arab aid." This fact is not denied by British historians and military writers; and the famous Lawrence of Arabia, who fought with his Arab friends in the war against Turkey, bears witness to its truth. Moreover, General Allenby himself stated that Arab help had been "invaluable" in winning the war.

In 1918, first Turkey's and then Bolshevik Russia's revelations of the secret agreements between France and England to divide up the Arab provinces of the Ottoman Empire, as also the Balfour Declaration promising a national home for the Jews in Palestine, caused such dismay and suspicion in the Arab armies that the British Government reiterated its former pledges.

In a communication sent to a meeting of Arab leaders in Cairo in June 1918, Britain publicly confirmed her earlier promises in more comprehensive and plainer terms than in the unpublished MacMahon-Husein correspondence, and without the former ambiguously worded reservations concerning French interests in Syria. In plain terms it stated:

(1) That with regard both to the territories which were free and independent before the War, and those liberated from Turkish rule by the Arabs themselves: "His Majesty's Government recognise the complete and sovereign independence of the Arabs inhabiting those territories and support them in their struggle for freedom."

(2) That with regard to the territories occupied by the Allied armies (which at that time included the greater part of Iraq, including Basra and Baghdad, and the southern half of Palestine inclusive of Jerusalem and Jaffa), His Majesty's Government's policy was "that the future government of those territories should be based on the principle of the consent of the governed."

(3) That as concerns the Arab lands still under Turkish rule

(which included the greater part of Syria and Mosul in Iraq) the British Government desired "that the oppressed peoples in these territories should obtain their freedom and independence."

These quotations are taken from the translation made from the Arabic text by George Antonius in *The Arab Awakening* (London: Hamish Hamilton, 1938). As the author writes in his authoritative book, this British "Declaration to the Seven," as it is usually called, committed Britain to her subsequently dishonored pledges more decisively than the MacMahon letters, since it was made public, and came both after Moscow's disclosure of the secret Sykes–Picot agreement with France and the Balfour Declaration.

The ambiguity of the Balfour Declaration, designed to enlist Zionist support without upsetting the Arabs, was the cause of all the subsequent trouble. While saying that His Majesty's Government would use its "best endeavors to facilitate" the "establishment in Palestine of a national home for the Jewish people," it also stated that it was to be "clearly understood that nothing shall be done which may prejudice the civil and religious rights of existing non-Jewish communities in Palestine." The Declaration could not therefore be held to envisage the establishment of a Jewish State in Palestine, and the British sent a special emissary to King Husein assuring him that it held no contradictions to the promises made to the Arabs.

Together with President Wilson's Fourteen Points, the twelfth of which promised that "nationalities which are now under Turkish rule" should be assured "an absolutely unmolested opportunity of autonomous development," these false British pledges dispelled Arab doubts and apprehensions, and led them to fight gallantly when General Allenby called upon them to participate in the final and victorious offensive which won the war in the Middle East.

Then came the great betrayal which forfeited the trust which the Arabs had formerly reposed in Britain and made them suspicious of all Western professions and promises. Britain, having won the war with the help of the Arabs, failed to honor her pledged word. Regarding her solemn engagements to the Arabs as scraps of paper worth little account in comparison with her 1916 secret Sykes-Picot agreement with France and her promise to the Zionists in the Balfour Declaration, England established her dominion over Iraq and Palestine, and let France forcibly convert Syria into a colony against the brutally repressed opposition of its inhabitants, under the same false pseudonym of League of Nations "mandated" territories.

Nor was Britain alone guilty of this flagrant breach of faith with the Arabs who had helped her to win the war. The French, it is true, knew nothing of the MacMahon-Husein correspondence, kept secret from them by Britain, who immediately after her pledges of Arab freedom and independence, negotiated her 1916 secret treaty with France to divide up these same Arab territories, thus double-crossing France as well as the Arabs. But the French associated themselves with Britain's dishonored promises when, in order to prevent a threatening Arab mutiny, a joint Anglo-French communication from their General Headquarters was issued on November 7, 1918, given wide publicity, and posted in all the towns and villages of Palestine, Syria and Iraq. In this proclamation the two Great Powers declared that their joint war aims were: "The complete and definite freeing of the peoples so long oppressed by the Turks, and the establishment of National Governments and Administrations deriving their authority from the initiative and the free choice of the native populations."

Even while Britain and France were thus acquiring a reputation for duplicity in the Arab world, Bolshevik Russia put on its disguise as the anti-colonialist friend of the oppressed peoples of the Middle East. Tsarist Russia had been a party to the Anglo-French plot to divide up the territories of the Ottoman Empire, although Russia was to have had only non-Arab territories. By publishing the secrets found in the Tsarist archives, by rejecting Russia's share of the Turkish spoils (which were to have included Constantinople), and by relinquishing the privileges and powers in China acquired by the Tsars, Communist Russia laid the groundwork for her claims to be non-imperialist in her dealings with the peoples of Asia, while Britain and France were left to reap the whirlwind sown by their betrayal of Arab hopes and expectations.

Today, with Moscow winning a strong foothold in the Middle East and assiduously wooing the Arab nationalists, the events of almost forty years ago are of more than historical importance. The betrayal of the pledges given to the Arabs by Britain and France was announced by the Supreme Council of the victorious Allied Powers at its meeting in St. Remo in April 1920. The Arab lands in the rectangle between the Mediterranean and the Persian frontier, instead of being given the freedom promised them, were to be placed under League of Nations "mandates"—a euphemism for Western colonial rule. Syria was to be broken up into three pieces: Palestine under Britain, Lebanon and a reduced Syria under France. Iraq was kept undivided but under a British mandate. The territories which now constitute Saudi Arabia were left free, thanks, no doubt, to the fact that in those days the oil riches of the Arabian Peninsula were unknown.

Intimations at the Paris Peace Conference that the Allies did not intend to fulfill their promises had impelled those Arab leaders who had drafted the Damascus Protocol in 1915 to organize elections to the first Arab Parliament which met in the Syrian capital in July 1919. This "All Syrian Congress" meeting in Damascus, which was then the heart of the Arab world, demanded an independent Syria within her historic boundaries including Palestine, and voted for the establishment of a constitutional monarchy with the Emir Feisal as king. It repudiated the Zionist claim to Palestine, but proclaimed itself in favor of decentralized rule to safeguard the rights of religious and racial minorities.

A generation later, the London *Economist* (November 17, 1956) would report that President Eisenhower's stand on Suez "electrified Asia and won a respect never previously enjoyed" by America. With some chagrin it should be remembered that back in 1919 the Resolutions of the General Syrian Congress closed with an affirmation of faith in "lofty principles proclaimed by President Wilson [which lead us to believe that] the determining consideration in the settlement of our own future will be the real desires of our own people." Many Arabs then, just as thirty-seven years later, looked to "the liberal American nation, who are known for their sincere and generous sympathy with the aspirations of weak nations, for help in the fulfillment of our hopes."

The Syrian Congress also reminded the Peace Conference, "We would not have risen against Turkish rule, under which we enjoyed civic and political privileges, as well as rights of representation, had it not been that the Turks denied us our rights to a national existence."

The famous Lawrence of Arabia seems to have realized all along that Britain intended to break her word; but, evidently conceived it his duty to England to exploit the trust reposed in him by his Arab friends to induce them to go on fighting. As he was to write subsequently in *The Seven Pillars of Wisdom:*

> If we won the war the promises to the Arabs were dead paper. Yet the Arab inspiration was our main tool in winning the Eastern war. So I assured them that England kept

her word in letter and spirit. In this comfort they performed their fine things but, of course, instead of being proud of what we did together I was continually and bitterly ashamed.

By breaking her pledged word, England forfeited her most priceless possession and started to dig her own grave as a Great Power. Long before her attack on Egypt in 1956, she had forfeited the respect and trust of the Arab world by her cynical double-dealing. As has been often proved before and since, what the Germans call *Realpolitik* is not realistic, but merely a postponment of the day of reckoning, increasing the price which ultimately has to be paid.

George Antonius did not live long enough to see the consequences in our time of the British betrayal of the Arabs. But, on the eve of World War II, he wrote that if Britain and France had not in 1919 imposed a settlement which violated both the promises specifically made to the Arabs, and the principles enunciated by the Allies as the foundations of the peace:

> Thousands of lives, millions of treasure and incalculable moral suffering and damage would have been avoided. The Iraq rising of 1920, the Syrian rebellion of 1925 and the repeated outbreaks in Palestine would not have occurred. For they were all the direct outcome of the various regimes which were wrongfully and forcibly imposed upon the Arabs in Iraq, Syria and Palestine in violation of the pledges which had brought them into the War. Whatever part subsidiary causes may have played, the underlying cause of all those upheavals, and of a good deal else that has clouded the natural friendliness of Arab to Englishman and Englishman to Arab, is to be sought in the bitterness and the revulsion of feeling which the post-War provisions engendered—and nowhere else. The Arabs felt that they had been betrayed, and betrayed by their best friend.

The appeals and resolutions presented to the Western Powers in 1919 by the Arab Parliament went unheeded by all of them except the United States, which sent the King-Crane Commission to the Middle East to investigate the Arab claims. This commission made recommendations supporting Arab aspirations—which, if they had not been disregarded by Britain and France, would have changed the course of history and prevented Soviet Russia from winning her present influence in the Middle East. Specifically, the King-Crane Commission favored the preservation of the unity of Syria including Palestine, but with autonomy for Lebanon within a Syrian State, spoke against giving any mandate to the French because of their unpopularity, and recommended that any British or United States mandates be limited in time. Moreover, the members of the Commission concluded after much study of the Zionist problem that the Zionists looked forward to a practically complete dispossession of the non-Jewish population, and that the Zionist program could not be carried out except by force and in gross violation of the rights of the Arab inhabitants and President Wilson's Fourteen Points.

In the Arab world the consequences of Western double-dealing are only now becoming apparent, and we still have a chance to retrieve our position. But in China we have already lost out. We lost not simply because of the Truman-Acheson-Marshall policy after World War II, which denied arms aid and political support to our loyal ally, the Nationalist Government of China, unless and until it would form a coalition government with Moscow's agents, the Chinese Communist Party. Nor only in consequence of the Yalta pledge given by Roosevelt and Churchill to Stalin that his demand for concessions in Manchuria enabling Russia to dominate China should be "unquestionably fulfilled"—a betrayal of a loyal ally by the West which matches its broken pledges to the Arabs in the 1914 war. Our defeat began, long, long ago, when, by failing to make concessions to the Chinese nationalist movement until it had allied itself with Soviet-Russia, the West opened the door to Communist subversion, and enabled the Kremlin to obtain a permanent base in China from which it was to conquer the whole country a quarter of a century later.

Because of what may happen now in the Middle East, unless the West learns and applies the lesson of its failure in the Far East, it is necessary here to give a brief account of what happened in the twenties, when the Chinese nationalists were confronted with much the same problems and temptations as the Arab world today.

Today Nasser and other Arab nationalists frequently express their fear of "international imperialism." If they know anything about China's experience, their fears are probably reinforced.

While China was not, like the Arab world, divided up among the Great Powers into colonies, protectorates, or mandated territories either before or after the 1914 war, her condition was hardly more enviable. On the contrary, as was demonstrated during the war, China was at the mercy of any militarist nation that chose to attack her while the other Great Powers were busy fighting each other. Consequently Japan took advantage of the war—and of her secret treaty with England giving her a free hand in China in order to bring her into the war against Germany—to step up the tempo of her aggression against China.

Unlike the Arabs during World War I, the Chinese had been given no specific assurances or definite commitments by England promising them freedom from imperialist domination. But they too had joined the side of the Allies and had placed their faith in President Wilson's Mount Vernon address on July 4 proclaiming that the post-war settlement would be based on "the free acceptance of the peoples concerned." They therefore expected that the Paris Peace Conference would annul the "Unequal Treaties" imposed on China by force during the previous century—which had given England, France, Germany, Russia, Japan and the United States the privileges and powers which they jointly upheld to keep China subject and powerless.

Those were the days when Chinese reformers and patriots, later to be seduced by Communism, exultantly proclaimed, in words similar to those of the Resolutions of the General Syrian Congress in the same period:

> Now that justice has triumphed over force, all people should clearly realise that force cannot be relied on and that justice cannot be ignored. The speeches of the American President, Woodrow Wilson, are noble and just. He is the best man in the world. His most important principles are national sovereignty, and the sovereignty of the people over the government.

Chen Tu-hsiu, who wrote these words in the December 1918 issue of *New Youth,* was the outstanding leader of the Chinese intellectuals and patriots who had turned to the West for inspiration and political ideas to reform and modernize China and restore her independence, dignity and security. A year later Chen Tu-hsiu and his followers were forming Communist groups in the main cities of China, preparatory to the foundation of the Communist Party of China in Shanghai on July 1, 1921.

The reason why is as simple as it is important for us to understand—if we are not to lose the Middle East as well as the Far East. Disillusionment with the West, which failed to apply its liberal principles to people described by Kipling as "the lesser breeds without the law," drove Chinese patriots either into the Communist camp or into a marriage of convenience with Moscow.

Instead of the bright hopes aroused by the United States President being realized, the Chinese Delegation at the Paris Peace Conference in 1919 had been told that Japan was to inherit Germany's forfeited imperial position in Shantung. Nothing effective was to be done either to stop Japanese encroachments on Chinese sovereignty as formulated in her "Twenty-one Demands" or to release China from the shackles on her sovereignty previously imposed by the Western Powers.

Thus, the failure of the Western Powers to apply their professed principles of self-determination and equality to weak, or colonial, peoples gave the Communists their opportunity to move in to conquer China from within, by much the same methods as they are now using in the Arab world.

In 1918–20 the Soviet Government voluntarily abrogated all the unequal treaties imposed upon China during the previous century by the Tsarist Government, as it also then repudiated the secret Skyes-Picot agreement to divide up the provinces of the Ottoman Empire between Russia, France and England. Moscow then offered China friendship and aid based on political equality just as, equally falsely, in furtherance of her own imperialist designs, she is today giving support to Arab nationalism.

The apparent contrast between Russia's actions and the unyielding attitudes of the Western Powers and Japan led Chinese conservatives and liberals as well as radicals to turn to Moscow as the only ally available in their struggle for the redemption of their country. Like some leaders of the Arab nationalist movement today, the Chinese nationalists in the twenties came to believe, not without reason, that without arms from Russia they could not hope to free their peoples from the pressures of the old colonial powers or from the menace of a militarist Asiatic neighbor with expansionist aims: Japan in the case of China yesterday, and Israel today in the Middle East. To the Chinese, then, as to the Arabs before the Suez War, Soviet Russia appeared as the only powerful ally available.

In 1919, campaigns of protest spread all over China with mass demonstrations of students and workers in the big cities demonstrating against the Versailles Peace Treaty and denouncing the pro-Japanese "Anfu clique" which controlled the Chinese Government in Peking. The strength of China's awakened national feeling was also demonstrated by a nation-wide boycott of Japanese goods, which eventually forced Tokyo, in 1922, to relinquish title to the territory which she had acquired by the Versailles Peace Treaty.

Moscow, then as now, was of course waiting to take advantage of the profound disillusionment with Western promises and professions among all classes.

As Mao Tse-tung was to write in 1940, in his book called *The New Democracy,* May 1919 was the turning point at which the Chinese Revolution "was transformed into a democratic revolution of the new type."

In January 1923, Dr. Sun and Soviet Russia's emissary, Adolf Joffe, reached an agreement for joint action on behalf of the Chinese national revolution. Their statement of January 26 specifically rejected Communism or Socialism for China. The alliance was clearly stated to be one only for the achievement of China's national unification and independence.

Russian arms, money, technical and political advisers began to pour into Canton to implement Moscow's promise that the national movement "could depend on the aid of Russia." Michael Borodin arrived in Canton in 1924 as the Soviet adviser to the Kuomintang. The young Communist Party of China was given the slogan, "All work to the Kuomintang," which was to be "the central force of the national revolution" and to "stand in the leading position."

Two years before Moscow made its first overtures to the Kuomintang Party, Dr. Sun Yat-sen had been elected President of the Republic of China in Canton by the rump of the Parliament called into being, but almost immediately dissolved, by the Peking Government.

Dr. Sun's influence and that of his Party extended all over China and was particularly strong among the overseas Chinese in Southeast Asia and the Philippines. But the authority of his government in Canton did not stretch beyond the confines of this southern city, and it was at the mercy of the mercenary troops it had hired. In 1922, Dr. Sun had been forced to flee from his "capital city" by the general in command of these troops. After he returned there with Michael Borodin he was easily persuaded by his Communist adviser that the Kuomintang must train a fighting force of its own of politically educated adherents to replace the mercenaries and overcome the armies of the war lords. Also that it must become a disciplined party, and organize a mass movement of workers and peasants if it were ever to achieve its aim of liberating and uniting China.

The subsequently famous Whampoa Military Academy was founded in 1924, supplied by Russia and staffed with Russian military instructors under the orders of Marshal Bluecher, the Commander of the Soviet Far Eastern Army who arrived in Canton under the alias of Galen. Its first Commandant was the young officer Chiang Kai-shek, who had studied at the Moscow Military Academy. Its political instructor was Chou En-lai, who as a student in Paris had helped found the French Communist Party. Its graduates were to form the backbone of the Chinese Nationalist armies. It also trained some of the officers of China's Red Army of the future. There is a story in China that years later, after the break between Chiang and the Communists, Chiang Kai-shek spared Chou's life after making him prisoner because of their former friendship at the Whampoa Military Academy.

With Borodin as mentor, the Kuomintang was reorganized on similar lines to the Bolshevik Party and proclaimed a program of reform for the workers and peasants which was a combination of Dr. Sun's liberal but vague "Three Principles" and the revolutionary land and labor platform of the Communists.

In his negotiations with Moscow's representatives, Dr. Sun had refused to permit the Chinese Communist Party to affiliate with the Kuomintang; but he allowed individual Communists to join on condition that they pledged themselves to be loyal to Koumintang principles and aims. This proviso made little if any difference since the Chinese Communists maintained their own Party organization, and since promises have never had any importance for Communists anywhere at any time. They were now placed in a better position to "bore from within" than they would have been as a minority party either affiliated to the Kuomintang or in opposition to it. Under its aegis they increased their numbers by leaps and bounds. They recruited many of the most active and capable young members of the Kuomintang into their own ranks. And since the "Organization Department" of the Kuomintang, engaged in creating a mass basis of popular support among the workers and peasants, was headed by a Communist until May 1926, the Chinese Communist Party developed from a small group of revolutionaries into the organizers of a mass movement. Communist Party membership, which had only been 1,500 in 1924, increased to 10,000 a few months later, and within a year multiplied fifty fold.

While advancing from strength to strength, the Communists did not conceal their true aims from anyone who took the trouble to read the resolutions of the Comintern or the Party literature. Here it was plainly stated that the Chinese Communist Party was collaborating with the Kuomintang with the object of revolutionizing its principles and tactics and "converting it into a workers and peasants party."

As Harold Isaacs, the best informed of Dr. Sun's Marxist critics, wrote in the unexpurgated English edition of his book *The Tragedy of the Chinese Revolution**:

> [Sun] hoped to evolve means of transforming Chinese Society peacefully and without convulsion after securing power for himself and his followers by purely military

* London: Secker and Warburg, 1938. The edition published in 1951 by the Stanford University Press was revised by the author after he ceased to be a Trotskyist.

> means. There was nothing in common between Sun Yat Sen's concept of democracy and the [Communist] idea of the direct conquest of political rights and liberties by the people.

The antagonism between the Western-influenced political philosophy and enduring Confucian ethics of Dr. Sun and the Marxist materialist philosophy of the Communists was as great as the antagonism between Islam and Communist atheism. Unfortunately, however, this fact does not constitute any safeguard against Communist conquest from within or without, since the Communists, like the devil in medieval legends, are adept at disguising themselves as angels or fair temptresses who lure mortals to destruction.

Dr. Sun, like so many Western as well as Asiatic liberals after him, although he denounced the theory of class war and repudiated the Marxists materialist interpretation of history, failed to realize that there was a fundamental cleavage in *aims,* as well as in philosophy and methods, between him and his Communist allies. Then as now, the Communists aimed at the destruction of Western Civilization and all its values. Dr. Sun and his generation of Chinese patriots, like the Arab national leaders today wanted, on the contrary, to enable their peoples to enjoy the benefits and freedoms of Western civilization by emancipating them from its economic and political domination. Like the Arabs, they would have grasped the hand of the West had it been extended in friendship; whereas the Communists, then as now, cannot be conciliated or won over, since their aim is the annihilation of all ethical concepts covering the nature of man and society.

Although the methods of the Communists in utilizing the Kuomintang to build up their own strength caused disquiet and resentment among its "bourgeois" or conservative members, Dr. Sun until the end of his life discouraged anti-Communist feelings, or the expression of them. He seems to have imagined that Moscow was genuinely supporting him and the Chinese Nationalist movement. Either he failed to understand the basic antagonism between his aims and those of the Communists; or like some Arab leaders today, he harbored the illusion that national liberation movements can become associates or allies of Soviet Russia without letting the Communists run the show.

Colonel Nasser and his supporters in Syria, Jordan and elsewhere in the Arab world, have not advanced nearly so far along the fatal road of collaboration with the Communists as Dr. Sun Yat-sen and his successor, Chiang Kai-shek, did from 1923 to 1927. Today in Egypt, in contrast to America, France and Israel, the Communist Party is outlawed and its members liable to fifteen years imprisonment, in spite of Soviet Russia's arms aid to Nasser's government. Instead of following the example of Sun Yat-sen, Nasser seems to have modeled his policy on that of Kemal Ataturk of Turkey, who managed to maintain friendly relations with Soviet Russia and receive the benefit of Kremlin backing during the first years of his rule, while suppressing the Communists in Turkey. However, the Soviet empire today is infinitely stronger than in the twenties, and this game therefore is much more dangerous and unlikely to succeed.

Colonel Nasser cannot, in any case, be accused of anything like the same degree of political naïvété as Dr. Sun—or such Americans as General Marshall, who a quarter of a century later, believed that Stalin could be relied upon to support Chiang Kai-shek's Government if Chiang would admit the Chinese Communist Party into a "coalition government."

Dr. Sun and his colleagues were under the illusion, shared by most Americans during World War II and by some Arab leaders today, that you can ally yourself militarily with Communist Russia to achieve your aims without danger of Communism destroying you from within or perverting your war aims into the opposite of what you intend. The Western Allies of World War II, in their anxiety to smash Germany at the least possible cost to themselves, ignored the old adage that when you sup with the devil you need a long spoon. Since the true face of Communism had not yet been revealed in the early twenties, Sun Yat-sen is less to blame than Roosevelt or Churchill a generation later. Sun was not even aware that he had invited the devil to sup with him.

No one eats with the devil if he can satisfy his hunger in better company. If we offer the bread of freedom and independence and the wine of hope to the Arabs, those of their leaders who want them to enter the Satanic realm of the Communists will lose all influence and power.

A British historian, G. F. Hudson (*The Far East in World Politics,* London, 1937), has described the four-year partnership of the Kuomintang and the Comintern as "a marriage of convenience in which each side hoped, first to make use of and then to cheat the other." Certainly the Communists saw it in that light and made no secret of their intention to liquidate the Kuomintang after having used it for their own revolutionary ends.

It is no doubt true that the Chinese bankers, merchants and contractors who gave financial backing to the Kuomintang similarly planned to use and then discard the Communists. The last thing they desired was a "dictatorship of the proletariat." But they realized that if the whole of China was to be won for the Kuomintang, it must obtain mass support by means of the demagogic propaganda which the Communists supplied, along with their ability and energy in organizing trade unions and peasant associations. The Communists for their part expected that, by ostensibly subordinating themselves to the Kuomintang, they would eventually ride to power on the crest of the wave of the national movement against imperialism and the popular reform movement promising "land to the tiller" and a new deal for the wretchedly poor and terribly exploited Chinese workers. And they would probably have succeeded in the twenties, instead of having to wait for three decades, had they not over-reached themselves, and if Chiang Kai-shek had not turned the tablcs against them in 1927.

Sun Yat-sen died on March 12, 1925. Chiang Kai-shek, who succeeded him as the leader of the Chinese Nationalist Party and Government, had greater practical political competence. Well aware of Communist designs, he prepared to meet fire with fire. He made his first strike against the Communists in 1926 by closing down their trade-union and strike committees, and by arresting the Communist Party's "political workers" attached to army units. But neither he nor Moscow were as yet ready for a show-down. Stalin suppressed the news of Chiang's crackdown on the Chinese Communists; and Chiang continued to profess admiration for the Comintern, saying that its two aims were to unite the oppressed peoples and the proletariat of the world.

The inevitable and complete break which began the Civil War came a year later, after the triumphant army of the Kuomintang–Communist coalition had swept from Canton to Shanghai in a series of almost bloodless victories. The mass support of millions of Chinese peasants, workers, coolies, small shopkeepers, landowners and students, imbued with patriotic fervor or hoping to improve their miserable conditions of life, caused the armies of the war lords to melt away or to join the Nationalists.

Shanghai was the citadel of Western financial and political influences, as well as the center of Chinese banking and merchant interests linked up with the Western "imperialists." The conservative, moderate or middle-class wing of the Kuomintang, led by Chiang Kai-shek, wanted to avoid a head-on clash with Britain, France and the United States, to negotiate for recognition and treaty revision, and to obtain Western financial assistance for the reformation and regeneration of China. The Communists wanted to expel the West from China by violence for the benefit of Soviet Russia and to prevent "the stabilization of the Chinese Revolution on a bourgeois basis."

Happily, Britain then had a government which realized that the only policy which could destroy the Communist power in Asia was an alliance with the moderate, Western-oriented Nationalist forces.

In contrast to Anthony Eden's unrealistic attempt in 1956 to crush Arab nationalism by force, the British Government in 1927 overruled the "Old China hands" in Hong Kong and Shanghai who demanded armed intervention against the Nationalist movement. Together with the United States, Britain cut the ground from under the feet of the Communists and their allies in the left-wing of the Kuomintang by offering far-reaching concessions: recognition of the National Government; treaty revision; tariff autonomy; cession of Britain's Hankow concession to Chinese sovereignty; and Chinese participation in the administration of the Shanghai International Settlement.

Stalin had made no secret of the fact that the Chinese Nationalists were to be exterminated once they had ceased to be useful to the Comintern. As late as April 5, 1927, in attempting to justify his unsuccessful double-faced China policy against his Trotskyist opponents, Stalin delivered a speech to the Communist Academy in which he said:

> Chiang Kai-shek is submitting to discipline. . . .
>
> The peasant needs an old worn-out jade as long as she is necessary. He does not drive her away. So it is with us. When the Right is of no more use to us, we will drive it away. At present we need the Right. It has capable people, who still direct the army and lead it against imperialists. Besides this, the people of the Right have relations with the generals of Chang Tso-lin and understand very well

> how to demoralize them and to induce them to pass over to the side of the revolution, bag and baggage without striking a blow. Also, they have connections with the rich merchants and can raise money from them. So they have to be utilized to the end, squeezed out like a lemon, and then flung away.

Unlike the leaders of the Western world who, during and after World War II, either did not know, or paid no attention to, the aims of the Communists as revealed in their literature, resolutions and speeches, Chiang knew what to expect. He decided to liquidate the Communists before they could liquidate him and the Kuomintang. Stalin's scheme to use the Chinese Nationalists against Britain, America and France while at the same time preparing to deny them the fruits of victory by a subsequent "proletarian revolution," backfired. Having utilized the mass movement led by the Communists to frighten the Western Powers sufficiently to force them to come to terms, Chiang Kai-shek turned around and destroyed his Communist allies. He became the squeezer instead of the lemon, and should go down in history as the only man who ever bested Stalin.

Chiang, on arrival at the gates of Shanghai, ordered the Communists and their working-class supporters in the city to surrender their arms. The Comintern representative, instructed by Stalin to avoid an open rupture, ordered them instead to bury their arms. Having been forbidden either to surrender or to fight, thousands of them were massacred by Chiang's forces, first in Shanghai, and later in Canton, after Stalin, caring nothing for the lives of his obedient followers, had ordered the Communists to stage an insurrection without any hope of success.

The trade unions were smashed for a generation, to the acclaim of the foreigners who, two decades later, were to denounce the Generalissimo as a "fascist dictator." Yet by that time

Chiang had developed qualities of statesmanship and restraint which led him to endeavor to conciliate his enemies instead of exterminating them. Perhaps the whole history of China in our era might have been different if, in 1927, he had been less brutal and had not alienated many true liberals by these massacres, not only of Communists but of trade unionists, students and peasants.

To Chiang Kai-shek in 1927 it may have seemed that he had no choice. The young Nationalist movement was menaced by powerful foreign foes who could, and would, have drowned the Kuomintang Revolution in blood and fire, in the same manner as they had crushed the Taipings and the Boxers in the past, if Chiang had not compromised with them. And he could not do so unless he destroyed the Communists and their influence over the left wing of the Kuomintang.

By becoming the squeezer instead of the lemon, Chiang Kai-shek saved his country for more than twenty years from becoming a Soviet satellite. But he incurred the enduring enmity, not only of the Kremlin, but also of the Communist fellow travelers and all the misled British and American liberals who followed in their train. Their influence in America and England, together with that of the British die-hards who hated the Chinese Nationalists more than the Communists, was to prove so powerful following the war against Japan and Germany that the United States withheld the arms aid and political support which would have enabled Chiang Kai-shek's Government to defeat the Chinese Communists and their masters in Moscow.

The fundamental issue in China in the twenties, as it is today in the Middle East, was whether the Nationalists would take the Moscow road of autarchic economic development under a dictatorship which would transform her into a replica of Soviet Russia, with peasants, workers and everyone else sacrificed to the process of creating industrial and military strength; *or* seek and obtain friendship and credits and technical aid from the West for progress in freedom. Britain in 1927 made it possible for China to take the latter course. Had it not been for Japan, the Nationalist Government would in all probability have been able to lift China out of her age-old poverty by means of Western aid and gradual reforms carried through without violence and expropriations. But its very success in the decade 1927-37 in overcoming the centrifugal forces, reforming the Administration and developing China's productive forces was the reason for Japan's full-scale attack in July 1937.

The eight-year-long Sino-Japanese War which began in 1937 ruined China. She fought longer and with far less aid than any other ally of America in World War II. Thanks to Japan, and to America's post-war policy, the Chinese Communists were given their second chance to convert their country into an appendage of the Soviet Empire. In 1949 they won the victory denied to them by Chiang Kai-shek in 1927.

But it was not Japanese aggression and United States policy alone which led finally to Communist victory. The root of the matter lay in the ill-omened partnership of the Nationalists and Communists back in 1922-27, when the generous fervor of Chinese patriots and idealists for liberty, social justice and the emancipation of their country was misused, perverted, or rendered abortive by the Comintern's double-faced cynical policies. Those who had joined or followed the lead of the Communist Party on the mistaken assumption that its aims were theirs were ruthlessly sacrificed by the Kremlin to its own ambitions—and just as ruthlessly, however necessarily, punished by Chiang Kai-shek.

Partnerships with Communism are not broken easily. Disassociation does not come as a mannerly disagreement between equals, but as the escape of a potential slave from his would-be master, accomplished usually only by violence. The violence of 1927 was the terrible price that China had to pay for the help she had received from Communism during the previous five years. The youth who died, or lost heart, or became time-servers in the days of wrath and vengeance, torture and death following the break with Moscow, were the flower of the nation. Never again would there be such high hopes, self-sacrifice and patriotic fervor as had been displayed in the brief period when men of all parties and classes had joined to raise China from the abject state into which she had fallen in the nineteenth century—and when they had been led astray by Communism. The experience of 1922-27 undermined Chinese idealism, weakened the will of the nation, and made it more difficult to resist the new attack in 1946.

It could happen again in the Middle East. The patriotic and progressive-minded Arab youth, unlike that of China in the twenties, has not been seduced by Communist ideas; it follows national leaders who enjoy their own mass support rendering them far more independent than the Kuomintang in the days of Sun Yat-sen. But if the West continues to exert economic and political pressure with the aim of isolating or destroying these leaders, self-preservation may drive them to take the China road; and present sentiments of gratitude toward Russia among the Arab peoples may be transformed into sympathy for Communism, leading to collaboration, and eventually, as with China, to disaster.

II

THE UNITED STATES VERSUS THE USSR IN THE MIDDLE EAST

What befell in China a generation ago, as briefly recounted in the preceding chapter, should help us to understand the situation in the Arab world today. Soviet Russia, following her repulse in Europe, has reverted to the Lenin line of undermining the West by supporting nationalist movements in Asia. And it would seem that Khrushchev and Bulganin, or whoever it is who now rules Russia, are avoiding Stalin's stupidities—in the too obvious double-dealing which caused the Kremlin failure in China in the twenties. Today one cannot find Communist publications or speeches by Russian leaders proclaiming that Nasser, or other leaders of Arab nationalism, will be thrown away like "squeezed lemons" when they have served the purpose of Soviet power. Now the Communists operate so subtly that suspicions are allayed. Instead of openly proclaiming their real aims, as in China in the twenties, they masquerade as Arab nationalists and, by voicing their complaints more loudly than anyone else, have apparently succeeded in infiltrating the press and radio and some governments. In these positions of vantage they stoke the fires of suspicion and resentment against the West in order to prevent understanding and reconciliation and the formation of an Arab-Western alliance against the Moscow-Peking axis. By identifying America with "Western imperialism," French colonial rule and Israel's expansive ambitions, the Communists and their dupes have been all too successful in diminishing or destroying the feelings of gratitude and respect evoked by Eisenhower's stand on Suez—unfortunately also diminished by our subsequent policy of "squeezing" Egypt economically and attempting to isolate her politically.

By giving the "Voice of the Arabs" a Communist coloring through its adoption of Moscow's clichés, the crypto-Communists who have apparently infiltrated the Egyptian and Syrian radio and press, or suborned those in control, have also succeeded in convincing many Americans that these countries are already in the Communist camp. At least, they have given substance to the misrepresentations of United States newspapers which continually refer to Egyptian and Communist influences in the Middle East as if they were one and the same thing. Confusion to the benefit of the Communists is worse confounded when we ourselves make no distinction between the term "anti-Western"—meaning anti-British or anti-French imperialism—and anti-American, thus identifying ourselves with French colonial rule and British imperialist claims.

Knowledge of the brutal realities of Communist rule and the menace of Soviet imperialism during the past decade should have made it impossible for the Russians to play the old game of utilizing and perverting nationalist liberation and reform movements for the greater glory and power of the Soviets. Now, with considerable help from the West, the Communists are surmounting the barrier. By disguising themselves as Arab nationalists, and taking advantage of our identification of Arab national aspirations with "anti-Western" sentiment, the Communists are successfully carrying out the instructions given to them by Lenin in 1920:

> All the Communist parties must assist the bourgeois-democratic liberation movement . . . and enter into an alliance with bourgeois democracy in colonial and backward countries, but must not merge with it.

As we have seen, Stalin in China during the twenties botched Lenin's formula for undermining the power of the "capitalist imperialist" West. He not only instructed the Chinese Communists to "merge" themselves in the Kuomintang; he also forewarned the Chinese Nationalists of what was in store for them by proclaiming that this merging was a Trojan-horse tactic designed to destroy them from within, after they had served their purpose of weakening the West.

Today, as Vice-President Nixon recognized on his return from his African tour in the spring of 1957, the Communists regard Africa and the Middle East "as important as China was to them 25 years ago." And, he might have added, Moscow is now playing a far more intelligent and subtle game; while England and France are failing to display the political sagacity of the British Government in 1926-27, when it split the Kuomintang–Communist coalition by coming to terms with what Marxists call "bourgeois nationalism."

Instead of foiling Moscow by recognizing the legitimate claims of the Arab nationalists and by helping them to develop into "bourgeois democracies" under reformist, modern-minded governments with popular support, England and France have endeavored to crush or weaken the Arab nationalists. France, by her use of NATO divisions and American arms and helicopters intended for the defense of Europe, has involved us in her foolish and futile effort to crush the Algerian Liberation forces.

And England, by joining France in the Suez War with the avowed aim of overthrowing Nasser, has revived Arab fears that "Western imperialism" is intent on reestablishing its domination over the Near and Middle East.

Thanks to Eisenhower's courageous and principled stand against aggression, even when committed by our allies, America won the confidence and respect of millions of Arabs and almost succeeded in closing the door to Russian propaganda and influence in the Middle East, which England and France opened wide. Together with the Eisenhower Doctrine promising arms and economic aid to the enemies of our enemies, the United States stand on Suez has secured us the support of some Arab governments. But the joint pressures of Britain, France, the Zionists and the American press, coupled with the intemperate, unwarranted, and Communist-colored attacks on America by the Cairo press and radio, hamper the State Department's endeavor to pursue a policy consonant with American principles and interests. Thus we have failed to spike the propaganda guns of the Communists, as we could have done by giving evidence of our readiness to help the basically Western-oriented, reformist or revolutionary elements in the Arab world, whose aspirations for freedom, independence, unity and opportunity are not dissimilar to those of our forefathers in 1776. Instead the United States is in danger of getting into the false position of having our interests, and those of the free world, identified with preservation of the *status quo* in lands which are not free, or in which political, economic and social changes are long overdue.

In the words of Constantine Brown (who, like most other American columnists and commentators, has damned Nasser as a Communist stooge), the kings we support in Jordan, Iraq and Saudi Arabia "represent an Arab way of life which is being increasingly challenged by the young, intellectual elements in the Moslem world . . . [who look upon them] as remnants of an ancient feudalism, whose rule must be ended if Arab peoples are to join the twentieth century."

This does not mean that enlightened Arab monarchs with American support cannot, just as easily as pseudo-representative parliamentary governments or popular dictators, institute reforms and guide their people toward economic progress and self-government. But it does mean that we shall play into the hands of the Communists if we shape our Middle Eastern policy on the assumption that it is seditious for popularly supported Arab nationalists to seek reform of the "feudal," tribal, or autocratic, monarchial arrangements of the past. If any king, sultan, sheik or ruling political clique can rely on receiving American aid by designating opposition demands for reform as "Communist inspired" or as a "plot of international Communism," we shall force even anti-Communist Arab patriots to turn to Moscow for help. We shall seem to give them no other choice.

Admittedly we are in a very difficult situation. Maintenance of the powers, privileges and perquisites of small ruling classes in the Arab world is not the final goal of American policy. We are upholding the upholders of the old social and political order only because they seem to be the only element which can be relied upon to be anti-Communist, since they must be anti-Communist to save themselves. But when we count upon them to assist us in undermining the power and influence of popular Arab leaders, who like Winston Churchill are prepared "to take the aid of the devil himself" to attain their national aims, we may succeed only in thwarting our own policy, by pushing the Arab world into Moscow's Satanic embrace.

The Israelis have not concealed their joy and amusement in observing what they regard as America's stepping into Britain's shoes in the Middle East. Writing from Jerusalem, in an article published in the June 1957 issue of *Commentary,* George Lichtheim says:

> It is nice, too, after all these years of American sermonizing about effete monarchies and retrograde European ideas, to watch the United States busy propping up the last few remnants of Arab traditionalism, and even taking credit for helping young Hussein of Jordan to disband a rebellious parliament! If the opposition leaders in Jordan and Syria were not so destitute of political intelligence, they could make something of this cleavage between Washington's abstract republicanism and the grotesque promises showered upon Hussein for behaving like a latter-day Stuart monarch.

Mr. Lichtheim is not, of course, opposed to America's policy of backing King Hussein, nor does he oppose the United States support of the government of Iraq, which he describes as a "royalist quasi-dictatorship," since these policies are designed to destroy Nasser's power and influence in the Arab world. He thinks that "the State Department's evident belief that royalism can still endure for a while is less unrealistic than its liberal critics tend to assume"; and he considers it very clever of the State Department to have "hit on the bright idea of denouncing Colonel Nasser's interference in Jordan as a manifestation of 'international Communism.' " This move, he writes, "was a distinct refinement upon Downing Street's traditional cunning." But he and other Israelis do not trouble to hide their *Schadenfreude* "at the speed with which American diplomats and correspondents in these parts have become converts to monarchy."

Nevertheless, while *Commentary's* correspondent in Jerusalem thinks it funny for the United States "to build upon such medieval relics as King Saud or the Hashemite dynasty in Baghdad and Amman," he does not consider it at all foolish: "the combination of King, army and traditionalists easily scattered the Parliamentary leaders"; and "royalist rule [in Jordan] turned out to be entirely practicable—as indeed it has for years proved in Iraq." He warns, however, that:

> When international Communism is described as the true cause of Jordan's troubles, the alarming thought suggests itself that those in authority who find it convenient to invoke this spectre have actually begun to believe their own propoganda; . . . If Washington is going to use slogans of this kind, it should do so with a clear consciousness that they are nonsensical."

These views must, of course, be taken with several grains of salt since the Zionists and their supporters are interested in discrediting all Arab governments as either reactionary or fascist or Communist influenced, and in representing Israel as the only progressive democratic force in the Middle East. Moreover, the idea that "the full force of the conservative bloc backed by the Sixth Fleet and the promise of financial aid" is a rock upon which American policy can safely be constructed ignores the main point—namely, that however reliably pro-Western a King Husein or a Nuri Pasha may be, there is no certainty that their successors will continue their policies, whereas Nasser is the agent of forces which will continue even if he is removed. As the London *Economist* says in its editorial of May 18, 1957:

> The momentary successes in the Middle East are being built on a few ruling cliques whose authority is not necessarily stable; convenient as these successes are, their political value may be fleeting. In the end it will be through Egypt that the West re-establishes contact with the main body of Arab nationalism, which, whether the rest of the world likes it or not, is an established fact of political life in the Middle East.

The end result of our endeavor to isolate Nasser and destroy him by economic pressure is likely to be as self-defeating as

Britain and France's old-fashioned imperialist "gunboat diplomacy." For, as the *Economist* also points out:

> There are cogent reasons for ceasing to hanker after the end of the Nasser regime. . . . People who know Egypt see no logical succession to it except chaos; and the most likely result would be the triumph of the Xenophobic left wing of the Army, or of an equally anti-Western Moslem brotherhood, or of both in alliance. . . . A working relationship with Middle Eastern Nationalism is at present impossible to the West unless it is on terms with Egypt.

Events in Syria during the summer of 1957 indicate what would be likely to follow the elimination of Nasser from the Egyptian political scene, namely a struggle for power between opposing factions with the pro-Soviet elements gaining the ascendancy. It was indeed ironical, and an unacknowledged admission of the false picture of Nasser presented in the American press, that at the height of the crisis the West looked to the Egyptian President to exert his influence to save Syria from becoming a Soviet satellite. As the *New York Times* correspondent, reporting from Damascus on August 25, wrote, President Al-Kuwatly would not give up his post to "vehemently anti-Western forces" so long as he was supported by President Nasser, "Arab Nationalist hero to the Syrians"; and that if Nasser were able "to maintain his own influence in Syria, President Al-Kuwatly may be able to steer his country down a middle political road."

Syria, according to the Middle East correspondent of the *Economist,* is a country where the fulfillment of the development schemes "achieved without a penny of foreign aid, bears witness to a sturdy, self-reliant economy"; and Aleppo and Damascus, according to the same and other objective Western observers, are as well or better planned and administered than any others in the Middle East. But political crises are as endemic as in France where, as in Syria, the Civil Service and the business world continue nevertheless to function. This would no longer be possible if the extremist, Communist-influenced elements won control, and Western oriented Syrians have told me that they wish they had a Nasser, or were under his rule. In Syria the young Army officers exert great influence and, according to an *Economist* report, "the real common denominator of their belief" is loyalty to "Egypt—or rather to the nationalist ideals of which President Nasser is the foremost spokesman." This means that so long as Egypt is at loggerheads with the West, and the Soviet bloc remains the only source of army supply, the Syrian Army will lean towards the East. But it can also mean that Nasser, who realizes the danger of too close association with Moscow, may be able to restrain this trend if we cease hampering his efforts or attempting to destroy him.

We should indeed be foolish were we to imagine that the friendship of a few Arab kings is worth the alienation of the millions who look to Nasser for a new deal for the Arab peoples. Such a loss cannot be compensated for: certainly not by the friendship of King Hussein of Jordan, whose power depends on loyal Bedouin sheiks of the desert, as against the Palestinian refugees who constitute the majority of the population; nor by that of his cousin, the King of Iraq, whose government, in spite of Premier Nuri Es-said's wise use of oil revenue for economic development, lacks popular support; not even by that of King Saud, who has wisely taken account of the sentiments of his people by maintaining friendly relations with Nasser. In the words of Dana Adams Schmidt in the June 18, 1957, issue of the *New York Times:*

> President Nasser still remains a popular symbol throughout the Arab world. *He symbolizes anti-Western nationalism, personal disinterestedness and a break with the corrupt past.*

> As popular symbols the three Kings, Hussein of Jordan, Faisal of Iraq, Saud of Saudi Arabia, are not in a class with President Nasser. Western gains are less impressive when President Nasser's power on the popular level is considered. *In Jordan especially, the pro-Nasser sentiments of the Palestinian refugees are kept at bay only by force of arms.* [Italics added.]

We misjudge the reasons for Nasser's popularity when we ascribe it simply to his having defied the hated or mistrusted "Western imperialism." The Egyptian "common man" sees the Egyptian President as his champion in the struggle against poverty, privilege, inequities, and governmental corruption—against all the barriers in the way of his betterment. Nasser's land reform, although not yet far advanced, is unmatched anywhere else in the Middle East, and he has given Egypt the first clean government she has known for centuries. His modest way of living, his private life untouched by scandal, his incorruptibility, sincerity and courage, and his personally democratic behavior increase his popularity and inspire trust.

The majority of the educated Arab youth, who like the Chinese students a generation ago exert a powerful influence, look to Nasser to fulfill their aspirations. And they are joined by countless others who long to modernize their countries and free their people from the hopeless poverty and shackles of the past, and to see the Arabs take their place as a reformed, independent and strong entity in the modern world. In a word, Nasser's influence and prestige are far too great to be destroyed by dollars given to his enemies or rivals.

The Romans, to whom the word "rex" (king) was abhorrent, appointed a trusted citizen with absolute powers in times of clear and present danger to the state and called him a dictator. It is in this sense, not in the ugly modern connotation of the word, that Nasser is a dictator, since he enjoys the trust of the great majority of Egyptians, as also of millions in the divided

Arab world. The proof that this is so is afforded by his behavior. Few if any other "dictators" in this modern world would dare to ride in an open car through huge crowds, as Nasser did even after his government had handed out weapons to thousands of civilians in Cairo and Port Said in order that they might resist the British and French invasion.

The Iraqi and Jordanian governments, which deserve the description "police state" or "military dictatorship," much more than Nasser's popularly supported rule, are rarely if ever abused and denounced in the American press. There is some justification to the Egyptian President's bitter remark: "They call me a dictator in America because I will not take orders from them. There are many dictators who obey the State Department, and they are not called names. If I obeyed their orders, the Americans would probably call me a good democrat."

Reading this I was reminded how, back in 1940, I heard Father Gannon, President of Fordham University, say sarcastically at a meeting in New York in support of China that Japan would no doubt be metamorphosed into a democracy overnight if she teamed up with the West.

If, as some think, Nasser is already boxed in by the Communists, or too far committed to them to retreat, then our only alternative is to help other leaders to fulfill Arab national aspirations by better means. Whether the Egyptian President is the heroic figure he appears to be in Arab eyes, or the villain of the piece, as he is represented to be in the American press, one thing is certain: No Arab national leader friendly to the West and free of guilt by association with Moscow can take Nasser's place so long as he is the only champion of Arab nationalism who wins widespread popular support throughout the Middle East.

Nuri Pasha is, no doubt, a wise and enlightened prime minister of his royal master's paternal, feudal rule in Iraq. Thanks to the Iraqui Government's collaboration with Britain and America, and to its utilization of a great part of its oil revenues for hydraulic and irrigation projects and other public works, it may soon raise the standard of living of all its people, as it has already done in the industrial field. The fact remains that the Iraqui Government rules by force, and it has never dared to emulate Nasser by challenging the vested interest of the great landowners who, far more than the mass of people, reap the benefit of the boosted industrial development. Moreover, efforts on our part to destroy Nasser by raising up Nuri Pasha, or any other Arab leader, are likely to be unavailing. The Arab rulers realize, even if we do not, the powerful demands for Arab solidarity which make impossible any bids for personal preeminence that threaten to divide the Arab world.

I was, unfortunately, unable to visit Iraq; but even had I done so I should have been unable to judge between the glowing reports of its progress and the opposition argument that, whatever the economic benefits of Nuri Pasha's policies, they will have little attraction in comparison with Nasser's revolutionary appeal to all Arabs to unite and jointly utilize their power, resources and wealth for the benefit of all.

As John C. Campbell writes in the April 1957 issue of *Foreign Affairs:*

> [Iraq's] isolation from its brother Arab states is unnatural and unlikely to be permanent. No other Arab state has been drawn into the Pact, and the pull of the Arab world is inherently stronger than that of the West. . . .
>
> America should help Iraq to hold firm, recognizing that it will remain with the West only if the West can find a sounder relationship with the rest of the Arab world. Otherwise the relationship becomes too heavy a burden for Iraq to carry. It also suffers some internal handicaps in realizing

> its potential for leadership of at least part of the Arab world. The fact that this potential exists makes it all the more important that Iraq achieve a peaceful transition from its present paternal and feudal rule to a system more securely based on the people, and to escape a position that finds it isolated in the Arab community and charged with infidelity to the sacred cause of Arab nationalism. . . .
>
> To command the winds [of Arab nationalism now blowing strong] to calm down is futile. . . . The only hopeful course is one which frankly admits Arab aspirations to self-determination, equality and independence, but sets limits to support of extreme claims which deny the rights of others.

Those who, regardless of the consequences, long to bring about Nasser's fall indulge in a lot of wishful thinking. It is, for instance, by no means certain, or even likely, that Saudi Arabia aims to isolate Egypt and Syria. On the contrary, there is much evidence that its aim is to unite, not divide, the Arab world. In fact, King Saud, although an old-fashioned monarch or tribal leader, appears to be a wise statesman who understands better than the West how to stymie the Communists. On the occasion of his visit to Baghdad in May 1957, he is reported to have said that although desiring closer relations with Iraq he would neither break with Egypt and Syria nor enter any four-power pact with Iraq, Jordan and Lebanon, because this "would only quicken the leftward trend of Egypt and Syria and split the Arab states into two camps" to the disadvantage of them all.

Homer Bigart, whose dispatches from Egypt to the *New York Times* have been remarkable for their objectivity and insight, reported from Baghdad on May 19, 1957, that it was "wishful thinking among the Western critics of President Nasser" to regard King Saud's visit to Iraq as signifying his estrangement from the Egyptian leader. Observers in Iraq, he wrote, "stress that despite King Saud's increasing anxiety over President Nasser's growing economic, military and ideological dependence on the Soviet Union, he believes the Egyptian leader can be brought back to moderation."

And the *Economist,* with its usual wisdom uncontaminated by wishful thinking, called attention in its June 22, 1957, issue to the fact that the communiqué issued after the Saud-Husein talks in Jordan, by its reaffirmation of the adherence of both kings to the "Solidarity Pact" with Egypt and Syria signed in 1955, "was a striking advertisement of King Saud's anxious wish to avoid a rupture with Egypt." Suggestions that the Saudi support for King Husein of Jordan "necessarily implied hostility to Egypt" were scotched by the *Economist* as due to "a misreading of Saudi policy." King Saud, to judge from the evidence available, including my conversations with his representatives in Washington, is still, in the words of the *Economist* "wedded to Arab nationalist policies of which President Nasser is the most powerful exponent."

It would seem that King Saud, far from using his influence and his oil revenues to split the Arab world, is endeavoring to heal the rifts. Like the Emir Husein, whom his father supplanted as ruler of the Hejaz and Keeper of the Holy Places of Islam, he might even emerge as the man to succeed in getting a common policy adopted by the Arabs from Iraq to Egypt and the Sudan. The fact that the Iraqui and Sudanese governments rallied to Egypt's support when she was attacked shows that this may not be so impossible as it seems.

Even if we could break the solidarity of the Arab world by raising up another leader in Nasser's place, is he actually so committed to the Communists that we should be justified in doing so? In my interview with him in December 1956, as also in my talks with informed American and European correspondents and with United States Embassy officers, I was persuaded that the Egyptian President is well aware of the danger of reliance on Russia and anxious to avoid becoming dependent on the Moscow-Peking axis for arms aid and political support.

We must realize that the West, far from helping Nasser combat Communism, has virtually presented him to Russia as a gift on the proverbial silver platter. Until 1955 all of the Arab rulers, including Nasser, refrained from establishing close relations with Russia, because they feared Communism. The change in attitude of Egypt and Syria was not simply due to their inability to secure arms from the West. It must at least in part be ascribed to the Geneva "Summit Conference" of that summer, when Soviet propaganda agencies distributed all over the world a photograph of Eisenhower and Bulganin sitting together and smiling in friendly intercourse. With Moscow spreading the idea that America and Russia were once again on friendly terms —and with the United States doing little to combat the notion— the Government of Egypt saw danger of renewed Soviet-American collaboration to the detriment of the Arabs, similar to that of the Truman Administration. Many Arabs felt that in their own interest they had better come to terms with the Soviet Power before they were sold out by the West.

In the words of Salvador de Madariaga, in the November 14, 1955, issue of the *Manchester Guardian:* "Colonel Nasser's new policy towards Moscow is the logical outcome of the new policy of Great Britain and the U.S. This new policy consists in coming to terms with the Soviet Union."

Striking while the iron was hot, David Shepilov, editor of *Pravda* (soon to become the Soviet Foreign Minister), came to Cairo in July 1955 and took advantage of the "Spirit of Geneva" to persuade the Arabs that they could safely regard Russia, not as a proselytizing Communist state, but simply as the one among several competitive Great Powers whose interests coincided with those of the Arab States.

Two English writers, Guy Wint and Peter Calvocoressi, describe in *Middle East Crisis* (Penguin Special, 1957) the atmosphere of September 1955 in which Egypt's fateful arms deal with the Soviets was consummated:

> They preached their doctrine at a favorable moment: feeling was so high that many Arabs would have called in Russia if Russia offered them help against Israel, even if it was at the full price of going Communist: many others took the easy course of persuading themselves that Russia really was a harmless ally. Russia was a long way off, had had nothing yet to do with Arabs, and had committed no atrocities against them; the Arabs were more than half inclined to believe that the adverse accounts of Communist oppression were Western propaganda. Even the more cautious and sceptical, like Nasser himself, felt that they could probably use Russia for Arab purposes, and that they could look after themselves and save themselves from Russian snares.

The April 1956 visit of Bulganin and Khrushchev to England, by arousing fears that a Soviet-British deal had been made, led to Nasser's recognition of Red China in July. Up to then Egypt had been in America's camp on this issue, instead of following the example of Britain, India, Pakistan, Burma, Indonesia and Israel. But the widely held belief in England that Sir Anthony Eden had come to a "gentleman's agreement" with his guests about the Middle East led Nasser to the conclusion that by becoming friendly with Communist China, one of the few countries ready to buy Egyptian cotton, he could counterbalance any Anglo-Russian deal at the expense of the Arabs.

In imagining that Communist China was independent of Russia, Nasser made the same mistake that many Western statesmen, politicians and writers were making and continue to make. And his belief or fear that Soviet Russia and England had made a co-existence deal giving Britain a free hand in the

Middle East was widely held in England at the time. Sir Anthony Eden himself evidently believed that he had come to some such "gentleman's agreement"—as was subsequently proved by the shock he sustained when the Soviets intervened in the Suez crisis. The British Prime Minister evidently interpreted the talks with his Soviet guests as meaning that if Nasser provoked Britain, she could deal with him without fearing Russian intervention, except by propaganda—or so he is reported to have assured his cabinet prior to Britain's attack on Egypt.

As the *New York Times* correspondent, Osgood Carruthers, reported from Cairo on May 18, 1957, Egypt has been desperately trying to stay in the middle "between the U.S. and the USSR." Mr. Carruthers also gave Nasser credit for having shown "restraint" toward the United States in spite of the strong political and economic pressures we have continued to exert against him, and our efforts "to isolate and subdue Nasser's Arab Nationalist movement."

Nasser must at least be credited with not being a hypocrite. When asked by Mr. William Attwood, in an interview published in *Look* magazine, June 25, 1957, to explain why, if he is not pro-Communist, Egypt abstained from voting on the United Nations resolution on Hungary, Nasser, instead of echoing Pandit Nehru's sanctimonious double-talk on the same issue, frankly stated:

> Because the Soviet Union was the only country in the Security Council that supported us in our dispute over the Suez Canal. We abstained out of gratitude.

In reply to a question concerning the extent of the Egyptian economy's tie-up with the Soviet bloc, he said:

> As much as it was tied to the Western bloc a few years ago. Is this an evil thing? We were down to one month's reserve of wheat last winter. We were short of petrol. We

needed to sell our cotton. We went to you, but you turned us down. So then the Russians sold us wheat and petrol. They bought our cotton. They helped us survive. Yes, and they helped us escape domination by the West. How can I say that this is evil?

Asked what he meant when he said that the United States, Britain and France are waging "an economic war" on Egypt, he replied:

> You froze our foreign currency; you refused to sell us wheat and medicines when we needed them; you tried to bring economic pressure on us to change our Canal policy. The difference between you and your allies is that they tried to kill us with bombs and you tried to kill us by "peaceful means"—by economic pressure and starvation. Both efforts have failed.

Questioned as to whether he was worried about Russia's economic and political penetration in the Middle East, he replied:

> Look—American logic is different from ours. The West would not trade with us, would not sell us arms, froze our assets—so what did you expect me to do? It was a question of life or death for Egypt.

Yet when asked whether he was still of the opinion he had expressed in September 1954, when he said that he thought Communist methods and tactics in all the Arab countries "are directed to stirring up disorder and hate," he replied in the affirmative:

> I still think their objectives are dangerous—and that is why the Communist Party is illegal in Egypt.

Politics, like life, is "a tragedy to those who feel and a comedy to those who think." It is one of the sad or funny paradoxes of our time that our policy in China a decade ago and the one we now seem to be pursuing in the Middle East, although aiming at precisely *opposite* results, are achieving the *same* results, because they are based on the same false premises. Today, as yesterday, the State Department tends to identify liberals and reformers with Russophiles or Communist fellow travellers, and to equate the desire for reform and progress as synonomous with willingness to collaborate with Communists. The difference is that now the State Department is *against* collaboration with Communists, whereas during the Truman-Acheson-Marshall regime, the Department was *for* collaboration—as witness General Marshall's January 1947 statement in which he identified "reactionaries" as those who refused to cooperate with the Communists and castigated them for their opposition "to almost every effort I have made to influence the formation of a genuine coalition government." In China a decade ago, America, hoping to help the liberals and reformers, helped the Communists to power by saying that it was liberal and progressive to collaborate with Communists. Today in the Middle East, hoping to destroy Communism, we label a non-Communist, progressive, and basically liberal Nationalist reform movement "Communist" and endeavor to frustrate or destroy it. Because we formerly regarded Communists as reformers, and now regard reformers as Communists, there is danger of achieving the same fatal results in the Middle East as in China.

In July 1946 the United States strengthened the Communists by giving them a sorely needed breathing space, when General Marshall placed an embargo on arms and ammunition exports to China in order to force Chiang Kai-shek to halt his successful offensive against the Chinese Communists and admit them into a "coalition government." Today, with the aim of preventing precisely the result which General Marshall endeavored to achieve in China in 1946-47—namely, a coalition between the Nationalists and the Communists—we are once again, by a reverse process, helping the Soviet Empire to extend its power and influence. By squeezing Egypt economically, and by announcing our intention to isolate her politically, we are in effect pressing Nasser into the Soviet camp, just as formerly, in the Truman-Marshall-Acheson era, we pressured Chiang Kai-shek to submit to Moscow.

Nasser has already been compelled by American and Anglo-French policies to rely more and more on Russia for trade and such aid as he can get. We have also succeeded in strengthening the influence of those anti-Western and anti-American elements which are so ignorant—or so blinded by their resentment—as to imagine that the Arab world can win independence, freedom, and strength through unity, by means of an alliance with the Moscow–Peking axis and its adherents in Asia led by Pandit Nehru. The only alternative to submission to Moscow which we seem to be offering Nasser is destruction at our hands.

Chiang was driven from the mainland because he remained loyal to his alliance with us even while we were undermining his government politically and denying him arms with which to fight the Communists. It remains to be seen whether Nasser, by pursuing an "anti-Western" policy, will come out of his struggle on two fronts better than Chiang, who acceded to American demands even though he knew that they were tragically mistaken and could only strengthen the Communists.

Certainly Nasser can look to the Turkish precedent as one which demonstrates that a national revolution in Asia has better chances of success if directed against the West, than if it relies on the West for aid and support.

In an illuminating article in the April 1957 issue of *Foreign Affairs,* John C. Campbell, Director of Political Studies of the Council on Foreign Relations, writes:

> The Turks went through their nationalist revolution a generation ago. It was directed largely against the West, and Soviet help was welcomed as a means of winning the fight. Turkey then went through a period of neutrality

> while it consolidated its independence, and finally turned to the West when it perceived the full implications of the Soviet threat. It is now willing to collaborate freely with selfconfidence and no psychopathic touchiness about "sovereignty."

The Kremlin originally denounced Nasser's regime as "reactionary, terrorist and demagogic"; and the Egyptian Communists were so convinced that the new government was beyond their influence that they "saw their best prospects in infiltration of the [dissolved and repressed] Wafd and the Moslem Brotherhood." Walter Z. Laqueur, whom I have here quoted, is certainly not a supporter of Nasser, whose government he designates as a "military junta"; but in Laqueur's article published in the *New Leader* on June 10, 1957, he shows that from 1953 until 1956:

> The Communists opposed virtually everything the junta did: Its agrarian reform was a sham; it was anti-labor; its foreign policy was pro-imperialist. The Communists gave their support to all the forces that opposed the junta, first the *Wafd,* then General Naguib in his quarrel with Nasser, finally the Moslem Brotherhood when it clashed with the junta. . . . The only serious competition with Communism in Egypt could come from a Kemalist regime, and the junta in those early years bore an uncomfortable resemblance to Kemalism. This danger receded only during the first half of 1955, when the junta finally decided to occupy itself with foreign policy rather than domestic reform. The attempt to establish an Egyptian co-prosperity sphere in the Middle East inevitably brought Colonel Nasser into collision with the West. He had to look for Soviet assistance, and he received it. The Communists thereupon changed their attitude, giving Nasser an increasing measure of support.

What Mr. Laqueur omits to mention in his illuminating article is the fact that the Egyptian Government's decision to "occupy itself with foreign policy" was a direct consequence of the Israel Army's attack on the Gaza Strip in March 1955. As President Nasser said to me, "Until then we hoped peace might be possible. But the attack made us realize we must have a strong army, and Israel, which had attacked us, was receiving arms from the West, especially from France, and the Herut Party had proclaimed that Israel's objective was to expand from the Nile to the Euphrates. Since the West denied us arms to defend ourselves, we bought them from Russia."

"Our fear of Israel," Nasser continued, "is on a smaller scale comparable to your fear of the atomic bomb."

I leave to a subsequent chapter consideration of the rights and wrongs of the Arab-Israeli conflict. Here I am concerned with it as the fundamental cause of the dangerous situation in the Middle East and its perversion of both American and Arab policies to the advantage of the Communists.

So far, Nasser has been able to resist the Western pressures impelling him toward an alliance with the Soviet Empire and to pursue an independent policy, thanks to the support of the majority of his people and his great popularity and influence all over the Arab world. But, as Wilton Wynn, the well-informed Arab-speaking head of the A.P. Bureau in Cairo, said to me in December 1956:

> The point has been reached in the Middle East when the victims of aggression feel that unless the United States really gives them support, they will be compelled to follow through to prevent the aggressors being rewarded. If, for instance, Israel is allowed to keep the Gaza Strip and part of the Sinai Peninsula facing the Gulf of Aqaba, the Arabs will feel that the Communist world is their only friend and will insist on calling upon Moscow for "volunteers" and arms. In that event, Nasser will be unable to face his own people if he continues to trust America and link his country's fate with the West.

Fortunately, the United States prevented this outcome by compelling Israel to withdraw her forces. Subsequently, however, we seem to have adopted a policy aimed at achieving the same ends by political and economic means as Britain, France and Israel failed to achieve by force.

Instead of helping and encouraging Nasser to come over to our side, the American press—even when it reports the evidence that he is trying to pull back from his close association with the Soviet bloc—would have us take advantage of this fact to tighten instead of loosen our economic and political squeeze on Egypt.

In order to understand Nasser's predicament, and to avoid driving him into an alliance with Moscow as the only alternative to being destroyed by the Communists or by the West, we must take account of the different political climate, or time-lag in experience, of Asia and Africa as compared with Europe and America.

In most Western countries, the illusions about Soviet Russia which perverted our policy during and after World War II have been dispelled by the ever-increasing evidence of the cruel contrast between Communist professions and practices. Few people in America or England, Belgium, Holland or the Scandinavian countries, practically none in Germany, and a diminishing number in Italy and France, are unaware that the Communist promise of heaven on earth for the "toiling masses," or anyone else, has not, and never can be fulfilled under the Communist totalitarian system which condemns most of its subjects to misery and want. The same is fortunately also true of the governments of the Islamic countries bordering on the Soviet Union, or close to it—notably Pakistan, Iran, Iraq and Turkey. And the people of Korea and Indochina, like the Free Chinese on Formosa, the two million refugees or escapees from Communist China in Hong Kong, and many of the overseas Chinese communities in Southeast Asia, know better than any Europeans or Americans (except the Germans, whose brothers are also under Communism's Iron Heel in Eastern Germany), the terror and misery and hopelessness of life under Communist rule. This is, however, not the case among other Asiatic or African peoples who, like Americans not so long ago, lack the knowledge gained by experience which is necessary to prevent them falling for Communist tricks—or, who imagine, like we did, that they can attain their national objectives by aligning themselves with Moscow. Since America and England grasped Stalin's blood-stained hand in order to force Germany to unconditional surrender; and since after the war we pushed China behind the Iron Curtain because we refused until too late to supply arms and political support to the Chinese Nationalists in their war against the Communists, we can hardly expect the Arab nationalists in Egypt, Syria or Jordan, struggling to achieve their national aims in face of Western opposition, to be more sophisticated or far-sighted than we were.

We learned our lesson too late to avoid giving the Communists dominion over Eastern Europe and China, although in time to erect a barrier against their further expansion in Europe. But today we keep on proclaiming that we are ready to let the Soviet empire keep its ill-gotten gains—thus sounding the death knell of hope among its captive peoples—if only the Communists will leave us in peace and cease from attempting to enslave more peoples. How, therefore, can we expect the Arab peoples, whose experience of aggression and foreign domination relates only to Europe and Turkey, and who have had no direct contact with Communist imperialism, to realize, better than we did, that in allying themselves with Moscow, or accepting her help to win their national objectives, they are digging their own graves?

The only way in which we can save the Middle East, or help it to save itself, from Communist domination is by understanding its problems and supporting the legitimate national aspirations of its peoples. Only thus shall we be able to enlighten the Arabs and enable them to resist the temptation to which we ourselves succumbed when we gave the Communists a free rein in Eastern Europe in order to defeat Germany. We should understand, or at least not deem ourselves superior to, those Arabs who are being impelled by their fears, passions, resentments and hopes to follow the precedent set by the Western Powers when we aligned ourselves with Communist Russia in order to liberate *our* "blood brothers" in Europe and smash Germany.

So far the Arabs, including Egypt's Nasser, have refrained from following our example. They have yet to make an alliance with the Soviet Power for the purpose of liberating the Algerians; or for securing justice for the refugees from Palestine; or for freeing themselves, as they see it, from the menace of Western-backed Israeli ambitions to expand. But, although the Communist Party is still officially banned in Egypt, those who have fallen under its influence are obviously exerting pressures which Nasser may eventually be unable to resist unless the West ceases compelling him to depend on Russia for survival.

No Arab government has so far emulated the Roosevelt Administration's kindness to Communists at home. Neither in Egypt nor Syria can one find government leaders endorsing the Soviet system, as Vice-President Henry Wallace did, when he told a monster gathering at Madison Square Garden that the Soviet "economic democracy" was in many respects superior to America's political democracy. Instead, the Egyptian Government continued to send Communists to prison even while receiving arms from Russia. Obviously, however, it will prove impossible for Nasser to curb the Egyptian extremists whose voice is often heard on the Cairo radio and in the press, or to avoid allying Egypt with Russia and China, unless America gives him some support.

To judge from the Egyptian radio and press, the Communists or their dupes are already exerting great influence. To an increasing extent the "Voice of the Arabs" sounds like the voice of Moscow or the voice of Peking. The Formosan riots which followed the acquittal by a United States court martial of an American sergeant who had shot and killed a Chinese, and the National Government's abject apologies, were seized upon as an example to "prove" that American aid "only serves to expose the country accepting it to the loss of its independence, whereby it becomes a puppet." This "so-called assistance," a Cairo broadcast continued, "is actually nothing more than a kind of imperialism, exploitation and domination."

Coupled with France's withdrawal of its promised aid to Tunisia, on account of the aid and comfort which this newly independent Arab state has been giving to the Algerians, the Formosa incident enabled the Cairo radio really to go to town. On May 27 it broadcast as follows:

> The people of Nationalist China have learned a lesson. In American eyes, their lives are but a trifling matter. Their government might be overthrown by a few chairs and window panes being broken in the American embassy by excited demonstrators. Sister Tunisia has also learned a lesson. Imperialists do not throw away their money, nor do they offer help out of love for what they call the underdeveloped peoples. Behind each dollar is a demand. Honor is injured and rights usurped. Will those concerned learn their lesson before they are overwhelmed by events and suffer the same fate as others before them? Will they miss the train of freedom, self-respect, and dignity?

Repeating Communist China's propaganda almost word for word, an article in the Egyptian newspaper *Ash-Shab* said that the Formosan riots demonstrated that, in spite of generous American aid to Nationalist China, the people of the island "occupied" by the United States "seek freedom first" and detest American policy because "American imperialism" has "cut off the island from the mainland, and transformed it into an imperialist bastion in the Far East." According to the Cairo broadcast of this article, the newspaper said:

> Strong ties bind Formosa's 9 million people under Chiang Kai-shek and the 600 million Chinese of the mainland. Since 1950 these 9 million Formosans have been closely following the progress of China and the cooperation and solidarity of the Afro-Asian bloc against imperialist plots and for the interests of nations and world peace. They themselves have been deprived of these things and compelled to be tied to America by a mutual security pact, which has resulted in the complete occupation of the island whereby it has become an atomic base for attacking the Chinese mainland. All this indicates that Formosa is heading toward liberation and unity with the Chinese people.

With a lack of gratitude or appreciation typical of the Communists, even America's pressure on Israel to evacuate Sinai and the Gaza Strip was utilized in a Cairo broadcast in Hebrew as evidence of "Israel's subjection to dollar domination."

It would indeed be strange if Egypt did not have its own Alger Hiss, and other crypto-Communists in influential positions in its government, press and radio. This does not, however, prove that it is already in the Communist camp, any more than America was during the war years when our press and radio eulogized Stalin's Russia, when anti-Communists were generally precluded from writing and speaking, and when many liberals swallowed and regurgitated Communist propaganda, just as the Egyptians are now doing.

The devil can quote scripture, and the ingredient of truth in the lying propaganda of the Communists makes the poison palatable to those who have a grievance against the West. Hence the success of the Communists in getting their misrepresentations of American policy accepted by those conditioned to believe it by their experience of western "colonialism."

The government of Pandit Nehru and the Indian press and radio, which are as controlled, if by more subtle means, as the Egyptian, continually voice the same Communist-inspired view of America. Moreover, the Indian Government has for years not only been on the most friendly terms with Communist China, but has also taken it at its own valuation as representative of the Chinese people and as a progressive and benevolent government, instead of as the brutal tyranny it is. All this did not prevent Mr. Nehru from being received with honor in Washington or from receiving American aid.

Lastly, in evaluating the significance of Egypt's intemperate attacks and falsifications, we should remember that the American press has been little less violent, unfair or untruthful in its attacks upon Nasser.

In addition to the power factor impelling some, but fortunately by no means all, of the Arab peoples to accept Moscow's help against "Western imperialism," we must also take account of the ideological factor. Communism, as practiced in the Soviet empire, no longer exerts the power of attraction it once had for Western liberal intellectuals and for their counterparts in Asian countries who have also learned how false are its pretensions to seek the welfare of the poor and oppressed everywhere in the world, and how brutal, miserable and poor is the condition of the peoples ruled over by the Soviet Government. But this disillusionment has not yet been communicated to Asiatic and African peoples who were long under British and French cultural influences which presented a rosy picture of the Soviet Union. Today, these same British, French—and also American—"liberal" influences have helped to give a new lease on life to the Communist myth by the support and praise they have given the Chinese Communist regime.

On my trip around the world last year, I observed the illusion spreading out among people from London to Singapore, Rangoon and New Delhi, and from there to the Middle East, that Communism *per se* is not evil. Now it is being said that Communism was perverted by Stalin or the Russians. Disillusionment with Communism, in both theory and practice, has been to a large extent prevented by the creation of a new myth. It is now widely believed in Asia, as in England, as also in some "liberal" circles in America, that the Chinese Communist tyranny has provided better conditions of life for the majority of the people. And even among the Chinese overseas communities who know better, thanks to the bitter experience of their relatives and friends in China, the Peking Government is given credit for having made China more respected and feared than any other Chinese government for many years.

Even the sophisticated, who know that the Chinese people are now in an even more miserable condition than before they succumbed to Communist domination, stress the undeniable fact that the Peking Government has been able to defy the West with impunity because of its alliance with, or subservience to, Soviet Russia. The Communist Government has got away with murder, both literally and figuratively, thanks to its being under Moscow's protection.

The Peking Government is both recognized and encouraged by our British allies, who announced in May 1957 that in spite of American objections, they would henceforth trade with Communist China as freely as they wished—thus repeating their past record when they supplied Japan with the sinews of war, until a year or two before Pearl Harbor.

The power factor is of primary importance in Asia and North Africa where so many people have been, or still are, subject to Western imperialist domination, imposed by force, and who still smart under the humiliation of being treated as inferior races. Communist China is regarded as having successfully defied America in Korea, thanks to our conclusion of an armistice, and few know the cost being paid by the Chinese people who have achieved "Great Power" status at the cost of slavery.

The Peking Government is given credit for having successfully demonstrated the military prowess of the Chinese people by defying the West. Thus even those who have been disillusioned by Communist practices in the Soviet Union regard Communist China with envy and admiration for her strength. Moreover, Communist China is still being represented by her Western admirers and dupes—and most powerfully by Britishers who are interested only in the immediate profits to be gained by trading with the enemy—as a shining example of good, clean, progressive and benevolent Communist rule.

Similarly, and with equally pernicious results, the Communist dictator of Yugoslavia has been helped, through generous American arms and economic aid, to propagate the myth that Communism *per se* is not evil and destructive of material welfare as well as liberty and that "national" Communist regimes can be our friends.

It is, however, not America but the British who, by the contrast between their attitude toward Egypt and China, have served notice on the world that all things are permissible to Communist countries, but that everyone else should beware of challenging the ageing British lion.

As I said in a lecture I gave to the Hong Kong Rotary Club in August 1956:

> After the Peking Government had expropriated a billion or so dollars worth of British property and investments in China, London told the Communists, "OK, let's forget and be friends! We shall jettison our ally, the Chinese National Government, recognize you, pressure Washington to do likewise, and do as much business with you as possible."
>
> But, when Egypt nationalized the Suez Canal with due compensation to the shareholders—following Britain's own example in the case of her mines and railways—the British

> cried, "Havoc!" and threatened war. In effect, they told Nasser, "You can't do that sort of thing; you are not a Communist; only countries under Moscow's protection can defy Britain or challenge her imperial interests!"

I concluded my speech by saying that Britain, by condoning Communist expropriation of her property in China and Eastern Europe, but threatening war against Egypt for having nationalized the Suez Canal was, in effect, advising the Arab world that it had better make haste to conclude an alliance with the Soviet Empire if it hoped to become master in its own house.

It was just eighteen years since I had last visited the beautiful and prosperous Crown Colony of Hong Kong. I had then been on my way to the front near Hankow and had hated to see the many ships unloading war materials destined for Japan, then in the second year of her war against China. Now the ships of many nations were openly or surreptiously supplying Communist China with the sinews of war via the same British "free port" of Hong Kong. Then, as now, the British (as also some Americans and unpatriotic Chinese in Hong Kong) were intent only on immediate profit. They were taking the cash and letting their political and moral credit go and, as before Pearl Harbor, unmindful of the fact that the lives of their own sons might be forfeited by their trading with the enemy in any future showdown with the Communist Powers. Instead they were chafing at the hindrances placed by America since the Korean War on their doing bigger and better business with the Communists. Meanwhile London continued to pressure Washington to follow its lead in abandoning the Chinese National Government and recognizing Red China.

Although in Korea Britain used her influence to hold us back from victory for fear that Russia would intervene, in the case of Egypt, where her imperial interests were challenged, the British Government was all too ready to risk a World War.

Today the British and their American supporters who damn Nasser as a Communist ally, agent or stooge for buying arms from the Soviet Empire, announce, as they did in June 1957, that henceforth they will supply the Chinese Communists with strategic materials in spite of the American embargo. Is it really more virtuous to help arm the Communists than to take arms from them? All in all it would not be surprising if Nasser were to conclude that the only way to induce Britain to be friendly is to ally Egypt with the Soviet Union.

It used to be said that we should not worry about China because Confucianism, combined with the individualism of her people, would prevent adherence to Marxist communism. So also today it is believed that the Islamic faith precludes adherence to Marxist materialist philosophy. These arguments ignore both the terrible compulsions which force everyone to conform once Communist rule is established and the temptations offered by Moscow to ensnare the unwary into its web.

Whether or not the Arab world joins our side or eventually succumbs to Moscow will depend on our policies and actions far more than on "ideological" beliefs.

Like China yesterday, the Arabs stand between the ageing, but not yet powerless "devils" of old-style imperialism and the deep unknown sea of Communism. The young, vigorous and dynamic state of Israel, with its Western-subsidized modern economy, is now playing a role in the Middle East not unlike that which Japan played in the Far East prior to Pearl Harbor.

Just as, when Israel attacked Egypt in October 1956, Britain and France rallied to her support, so also back in 1931, when Japan seized Manchuria, and again in 1937 when Tokyo launched her all-out war on China, powerful British interests in Shanghai, Hong Kong and London could not forbear to cheer. They were foolish enough to imagine that England would be enabled to regain or retain imperialist rights and privileges in China if the Japanese "taught a lesson" to the "uppity" Chinese Nationalists. Similarly in November 1956, Eden and Mollet thought they could set the clock back by supporting Israeli aggression in their attack on Egypt.

Nor does the analogy stop here. During the first years of Japan's war on China, the British Empire and the United States, instead of embargoing war materials to the aggressor, sold Japan all she required, leaving the ill-armed Chinese Nationalists to depend on Russia and Germany for arms and military instructors. Similarly today, France fights the Algerian Army of Liberation with American-supplied NATO armaments, and Israel—regarded by the Arabs as the spearhead of Western imperialism because she is subsidized by American funds—threatens to deprive the Arabs of yet more territory and render more millions of them homeless and destitute. Although Arab fears are no doubt exaggerated, it is a fact that Israel today, like Japan and Germany yesterday, proclaims her need of more *Lebensraum* to accommodate all the Jews she is striving to "ingather" from all over the world.

Despite President Eisenhower's refusal to condone the Anglo-French-Israeli attack on Egypt, Arabs are still distrustful of the West. Not only Nasser, but many other Arab nationalists see no reason why, so long as America continues to subsidize and arm Israel and France, they should not take arms aid and technical assistance from Moscow if this is the only source of supply available.

As an Egyptian said to me in Cairo:

> No one called Churchill or Roosevelt a Communist puppet, stooge or agent, when they *gave* Communist Russia the arms which enabled her to defeat Germany and impose her tyranny over Eastern Europe. We have merely bought arms from Russia for the purpose of defending ourselves against aggression. Why therefore should we be

accused of being pro-Communist and anti-Western? Is it really worse to buy arms from the Communists than to give them arms as you did?

The favorite quotation of the sophisticated Arabs of both the Christian and Moslem faiths whom I met in Cairo, Port Said, Beirut, Jerusalem and Bethlehem, was Winston Churchill's wartime statement that he would "take the aid of the devil himself" to save England. Why, they asked, should Nasser be called a Communist agent or puppet because he bought arms from the Soviet Empire, while Churchill, who at Teheran and Yalta agreed to deliver millions of Europeans to Communist slavery in order to "win the war" against Germany, is regarded as a great English statesman?

Why, indeed, should there be a double standard in judging the British Empire and the Arab world?

It was also frequently pointed out to me that the West never judged Israel and the Arabs by the same yardstick. Nasser was smeared in the American press as an ally of the Soviet Union because he obtained arms from Czechoslovakia; but no such accusation was levelled against the State of Israel which, in 1948, was largely indebted for her victory over the Arabs to "timely and substantial shipments of arms from behind the Iron Curtain, primarily from Czechoslovakia."

Many other examples could be cited of our double-standard judgments. England and France, for instance, can invite Soviet dancers, musicians, football teams, show Russian movies, and otherwise foster "cultural" contacts with the Soviet Empire with no unfavorable reactions from the United States. But when Egypt starts doing the same thing, it is taken as evidence of her "anti-Western" orientation.

Britain in her quest for profit, or in order to maintain the comparatively high standard of living to which her people are accustomed, unilaterally announces her resumption of exports of strategic war materials to Communist China; and America, while regretting this betrayal of our prisoners in China and the help it gives to the enemies of the free world, condones Britain's action saying: "Poor Britain, she surely has to trade with the enemy to keep going, so don't let's make a fuss." But when Egypt, in her endeavor to escape from the economic squeeze to which she is being subjected by the West, and in order to provide food for her starving people, enters into commercial relations with Communist countries, this is taken as evidence that she has teamed up with Moscow.

Nor can the Arab nationalist leaders have failed to take note of the fact that America is continuing to supply huge quantities of arms and economic aid to the Communist dictator of Yugoslavia, in spite of Marshal Tito's statement that in the event of war he would stand shoulder to shoulder with his Russian comrades. The contrast between our wooing of Tito and our cold-shouldering of Nasser—who, in contrast to the Yugoslav dictator is not ideologically allied with Moscow—is hard for the Arabs to understand. They can only assume that the United States is "colonial minded" and therefore applies standards to Europeans different from those she feels suited to Asiatics or Africans.

Certainly, even to less "simple minded" people than the Arabs, our unconditional aid to Tito seems to make nonsense of our claim to be engaged in a worldwide struggle against Communism.

Britain's eagerness to do business with Red China, our readiness to help a Tito or a Gromulka, and our aid to Nehru, whose "neutrality" favors the Moscow-Peking Axis, have created the impression that nations closely aligned to Moscow, or with influential Communist parties urging them to commit themselves to the Communist camp, get better treatment from the West than our friends and allies in Asia and Africa among the newly independent nations, or those still struggling to be free.

The *New York Times* of May 11, 1957, reports these words of President Habib Bourguiba of Tunisia, one of the staunchest supporters of the United States in the Arab World:

> Curing the Communist evil after it had reached critical proportions was more important to the United States than preventive expenditures in countries whose governments had chosen unequivocal alliance with the free world. Thus the U.S. was putting a financial premium on flirtation with the Communists.

Unfortunately for Egypt, "flirtations with Moscow" fail to produce ardent advances from the United States when these would conflict with America's faithfulness to England and France. Moreover, since none of the Arab countries can in any case compete with France as regards the number and influence of their Communist parties, Paris usually wins in any argument as to where most help should be given by America. Thus, France, where one in four of the population votes Communist, receives generous aid from the United States—which she uses to suppress the Algerian liberation forces, who reject Communist help.

Meanwhile Moscow continues to win friends and influence people in the Middle East by pretending to favor Arab independence, and by supplying her small quota of economic aid or arms without any obvious strings attached. Even when, as during the Suez War, the United States dares to resist Zionist pressures in America and acts boldly and wisely in opposition to the imperialist interests of Britain and France, the necessity to cushion the blow to our Anglo-French allies, or to reconcile ill-informed American public opinion, forces a retreat which sacrifices the fruits of our moral victory and strengthens Communist influence.

Having witnessed last December in Jordan, Lebanon and Egypt the joyful surprise and gratitude evoked by America's stand on the Suez War, I am convinced that we could have won, and still could win, the loyal support of the greater part of the Arab world in our struggle against Soviet imperialism, if we would persist in standing for equal justice for all, and in opposition to aggression even when the culprits are our allies.

Instead, Israel, although slapped down for her attack on Egypt, continues to receive tax-free American dollars collected by Zionist organizations and as early as March 1957 was promised restoration of United States Government dollar aid while Egypt's own dollar assets were still being frozen in the United States. Moreover, the United States refused to give or sell even food, medical supplies, or blankets to the bombed-out population of Port Said, even when requested to do so by church organizations.

Meanwhile Russia in an ostentatious gesture of generosity was supplying the food and medical supplies denied by America to starving and homeless Egyptians.

Our attitude toward Egypt can be likened to that of a stepmother who, forced by her principles to chastise her own children for beating up their stepbrother, also punishes the victim by putting him on a diet of bread and water. Thus America after September 1956 even cut off the shipments of our surplus food which had formerly been given to CARE for distribution to hungry Egyptian school children. As Senator Hubert Humphrey stated on May 2, 1957, at a press conference during his visit to Cairo: "It is not good for Americans to have any nation feel we use food as a weapon for political reprisal and political discipline . . . the food program should be reestablished quickly on our initiative. We should not be petty."

The Democratic Senator from Minnesota also stated that "Egypt is not hostile to us" and that, although Nasser feels we are trying to isolate him and put economic pressure on him so that he won't last, he is "unhappy but not bitter about America's reactions." However, as Senator Humphrey was wise enough to perceive: "He could become bitter and his bitterness could lead to very irrational acts on his part injurious to the peace of the entire area."

A month later, as revealed in his interview with *Look's* correspondent, quoted earlier in this chapter, Colonel Nasser had become bitter:

> I've been giving Americans my opinions about the Middle East for five years. It hasn't done any good. As I said before, I'm fed up. All I will say is that we are at a turning point in our relations with the West. I would suggest that you Americans try to get accurate information about this part of the world. Don't be superficial. It is to your own interest to understand the character of the Middle East. . . .
>
> Would you trust someone who is stalking you with a gun? We were attacked by your British and French allies. We were threatened by Dulles. I read what they call me in the American press. What I am saying is, you make it hard for me to trust you.

I became convinced during my hour's interview with President Nasser on December 19, 1956, that he is not anti-Western. But since then we have certainly made it hard for Nasser to restrain those who are, without his becoming a Chiang Kai-shek attacked by both sides.

Moscow originally backed Israel, thereby winning the support of many Jews everywhere in the world and particularly in America. She would surely do so again, should Nasser follow the example of the Chinese Nationalist leader and commit himself unequivocally to the West.

Nasser probably knows little or nothing about China. But the lesson her tragic fate teaches must have been borne in on the Egyptian President last fall, when, following his November 9th speech giving credit to the United States for having saved Egypt from the Anglo-French-Israeli attack, Moscow voiced its displeasure. According to the November 17, 1957, London *Econo-*

mist, (which was more fair and far better informed than most of the American press in its recording and editorial comment on the Suez crisis), both *Pravda* and Russian broadcasts were mad at Nasser for having thanked America, in his speech of November 9, for halting Anglo-French-Israeli aggression, instead of giving Russia all the credit.

Today, no doubt as a result of what Nasser has described as "the war of hate and nerves against Egypt which succeeded armed aggression," he is now more circumspect. Speaking in Alexandria on July 27, 1957, the Egyptian President, like the United States Ambassador to Paris last November, said that Britain and France had accepted the cease fire because of Russia's ultimatum: "to save themselves from atomic war."

If the United States, instead of attempting to "discipline" Nasser even while protecting his country from Britain, France and Israel, had shown understanding sympathy and generosity for Arab aspirations and Egypt's problems, there is little doubt that we should have stymied, instead of merely checked, Moscow's plan to bring the Arab world into her camp. Instead we have been frittering away the huge capital we gained by our stand on Suez.

As a result, no doubt, of the powerful pressure of the combined forces of Zionist, French and British influence in America, the United States Administration early in 1957 appeared to be receding from the bold and enlightened stand it took in the United Nations in 1956. Americans can continue to believe, or hope, that President Eisenhower, having dared to risk defeat in the 1956 election by his principled and enlightened stand on Suez, will not revert to the old fatal policy of entangling American policy with French or British imperialist interests, or with Zionist ambitions. But the Arabs, who cannot be expected to know or understand the complications of American politics, naturally judge "Western" professions by "Western" performance. And we ourselves confuse the issue by the tendency of the American press to identify both the opposition of the Arab peoples to French or British colonial rule, and their fear of Israel's expansionist policy, with "anti-Western" or pro-Communist sentiment.

This is analogous to describing the American Revolution as having been inspired by "anti-British" sentiment, or as instigated by the French monarchy, which helped the American colonies in their struggle for independence.

The important point is that when we treat as a Communist conspiracy the struggle of the Arab peoples for strength through unity, for liberation from French colonial rule in Algeria, and for freedom from fear of the re-establishment of Western European domination or of Israeli expansion, we play into Moscow's hand. By identifying liberal Arab aspirations with Communism we ourselves strengthen its influence and give substance to its false professions. Thus—in spite of our generosity and our good intentions—our tie-up with French colonialism, our aid to Israel, and our support of unpopular governments render us suspect in Arab eyes.

We appear to be offering not bread but a stone. The Communists, whose practices bear far less relation to their professions than ours, cash in on our failure to pursue a consistently principled policy independent of the claims and clamor of England, France and Israel. Consequently it should not surprise us if Arab national leaders who want to be, and should be, our friends, turn to Moscow in despair of ever winning independence, unity, freedom and equality on our side.

The Arab national leaders are for the most part men educated in British, French or American schools, colleges and universities, where they became enamored of Western ideas of liberty and justice. They were also made aware by their education of the possibilities for progress and prosperity in their own poor and backward homelands, by means of economic, social and political reforms which would sweep away the old tribal or feudal social structure and substitute popular government for autocratic monarchies or sheikdoms, or corrupt and oppressive bureaucracies. But although they long to belong to our world, the Western Powers seem always to be denying them the possibility of putting into practice the ideas they learned from us. Hence, the danger that they will succumb to the lure of Communism. The danger is increased by the fact that Egypt and Syria, against whom our pressures are being exerted, are culturally more advanced than the other Arab countries, with the exception of Lebanon.

In the twenties Stalin's rough and crude methods defeated Communism's purpose. Today cleverer and more subtle men rule the vast Soviet Empire, which now extends over China. Today there is no one in the Kremlin proclaiming that the Communists are utilizing national liberation movements in Asia or Africa for their own ends. Moscow's left hand is now so carefully hidden that neither Americans nor Arabs perceive that the Communists are undermining those they profess to support, as well as misleading the West by plots, conspiracies or popular demonstrations designed to divide and soften up the Arab world for Communist conquest.

Today we know far more about Communist aims and methods than during and after World War II, when we snatched defeat out of the jaws of victory by our trust in Soviet Russia. But we still fail to realize how devious and double-faced, how Machiavellian, Soviet policy can be. In particular, we never seem to realize that the Kremlin is adept at working both sides of the street in its all too successful efforts to divide and rule.

Just as while persecuting the Jews in Russia and its satellite countries Stalin stood as godfather together with Truman at the birth of Israel in 1948, so today, while backing Arab nationalism against Zionism, Moscow's hidden hand is busy promoting plots to sow dissension among the Arabs, and between them and Israel, in order that the "vacuum" in the Middle East shall not be filled by a strong federation of Arab States, but by the Communist Power. And since the United States, in its fear that Arab nationalists are, or must become, friendly to Moscow, is also pursuing policies fostering Arab disunity, the game is made all too easy for Moscow to win. Because we fail to realize that our best hope of preventing the Middle East from being engulfed in the Soviet ocean is to help the nationalists to establish an independent and viable federation of Arab States, we are helping to bring about the very thing we fear.

III

BACKGROUND TO SUEZ

Rarely has any issue been so obscured by prejudice and passion, ignorance, misinformation and malice, as the Suez Canal controversy. Those who denounced Nasser most vehemently as a violator of treaties and offender against international law did not deem it necessary to ascertain the facts or preferred not to know them. Instead of studying the terms of the treaties and conventions which the Egyptian President was held guilty of violating, the majority of American editorial writers, columnists and commentators of the right, left and center, spluttered with indignation and engaged in vituperation instead of argument. Old Guard Republicans to whom "nationalization" signifies "creeping socialism," which they deem more dangerous than Communism, reacted like bulls confronted with a red flag. "Liberals," who would no doubt have hailed Nasser's nationalization decree as a sign of his "progressive" policies, had he not been an enemy of Israel, similarly poured out the vials of their wrath against the "Arab Hitler" or the "dictator on the Nile." The Anglophiles and Francophiles swelled the chorus.

Former fellow travelers and friends of the Soviet Union, suspected of still being soft on Communism, welcomed the opportunity to cover themselves with whitewash by denouncing Nasser as a Communist puppet, stooge or agent. "Progressives" and "conservatives"; followers of Truman and Stevenson, together with Senator McCarthy and his adherents; columnists such as George Sokolsky and Henry Hazlett, together with Stewart Alsop, Marquis Childs, Drew Pearson and Max Lerner—all vied in the vehemence of their denunciation and abuse of "that man" Nasser. William F. Buckley's *National Review* and Frank Hanighen's newsletter, *Human Events* which, on almost every other issue, would have disassociated themselves from the *New York Times* and the *New York Post,* found themselves in general agreement with these newspapers. Only occasionally could the still, small voice of reason and truth be heard above the din of denunciation. The Scripps-Howard chain of newspapers, the Luce publications upon occasion, an odd conservative commentator such as John T. Flynn, a few real liberals and internationalists as distinct from the phony brand—notably Norman Thomas and Dorothy Thompson—and a few brave reporters such as Marguerite Higgins of the New York *Herald Tribune,* Homer Bigart of the *New York Times,* and Wilton Wynn of the Associated Press, endeavored to enlighten the American public concerning the facts. But their voices were almost drowned out. With the greatest degree of unanimity known in America since World War II, when conservatives and "reactionaries" joined liberals and "progressives" in grasping Stalin's hand in order to force the Germans to surrender unconditionally, the American press accused Nasser of having seized, grabbed, stolen or expropriated the Suez Canal, branded him a "proved treaty breaker leagued with the Communists," as "an unscrupulous dictator backed and actively supported by Moscow," as an "Arab Hitler," and so on and so forth.

Like Chiang Kai-shek a decade ago, Nasser got the full smear treatment—only this time the smear came from both sides. In both cases the result was to obscure the facts from the American people and strengthen the Communists. The important difference was that whereas the United States Administration had helped to undermine the Chinese Nationalist Government and make way for the Communists, in the case of Egypt the Administration strove to be fair and objective and thus avoid pushing the Arab world into Moscow's arms—in spite of the ignorant or prejudiced clamor in the American press and Congress.

Most editorial writers, columnists and commentators confused the Suez issue by making no distinction between nationalization of the status of the Suez Canal Company and observance of the Constantinople Convention of 1888, which are in fact two separate and distinct issues. As the State Department made clear at the time, Nasser's nationalization decree had not given any indication on Egypt's part of intending to flout the Convention by ceasing to operate the Canal as an international waterway. Alfred Lilienthal in his book *There Goes the Middle East* (New York: Devin-Adair, 1957) quotes one Administration source as declaring:

> There is no doubt that Egypt has the right, if it wishes, to nationalize the Suez Canal Company, assuming that adequate payments are made. If Nasser does not go further and does not disrupt the operation of the Canal, then everything will be all right.

No one who examines the juridical evidence and the historical record can legitimately accuse Nasser of having broken any treaty, or contravened international law, when his government nationalized the Suez Canal Company and started to operate the Canal itself. Reprehensible or not, this action was as legal as that of the British Labour Government in nationalizing British mines and railways and the steel industry. For the primary fact, ignored or denied by Nasser's enemies and critics, is that *the Suez Canal Company is an Egyptian company, incorporated under Egyptian law, which was given a concession to operate a canal running through Egyptian territory, which had been built by Egyptian labor.*

Far from having emulated Stalin's, Tito's, or the Chinese Communist Government's confiscation without compensation of foreign assets and the property of their own nationals, the Egyptian Government undertook to pay full compensation to the shareholders of the Suez Canal Company, at the price of their shares on the Paris Bourse on the day preceding the nationalization decree.

In the words of James P. O'Donnell in his article in the January 26, 1957, issue of *The Saturday Evening Post:* "In comparison with certain other statesmen who have been performing on the world stage, the Colonel seems to be Abdul Légalité."

If anyone doubts that the Suez Canal is Egyptian, not foreign, property and that it is therefore incorrect to accuse Nasser of being "a lawless treaty breaker," he need only look up the terms of Egypt's original concession to the Suez Canal Company, as also the legal arguments presented by the British themselves, when they enjoyed a "Protectorate" over Egypt.

When Egypt gave a concession to the Universal Suez Maritime Canal Company to construct and operate a canal linking the Mediterranean with the Red Sea, she was a part of the Ottoman Empire, and the Turkish Government, as a prerequisite to its approval of the concession to the Suez Canal Company, insisted upon clarification of its status.

This was accomplished by an agreement signed on February

22, 1866, "determining the final terms as ratified by the Sublime Porte."

Article 16 of this document reads:

> Since the Universal Company of the Maritime Suez Canal Company is an Egyptian Company, it remains subject to the laws and usages of the country.

The same paragraph states that disputes between the Company and the Egyptian Government must be "referred to the Egyptian judiciary and settled according to Egyptian law." It is also stated:

> As regards the disputes that arise in Egypt between the Company and individuals of whatever nationality, these must be referred to Egyptian courts, and their procedure be subject to Egyptian law, usages and treaties.

The only exception made concerns the "constitution" of the Company and "the relation of shareholders among themselves." These, "in virtue of a special convention," were to be "governed by the laws regulating joint stock companies" referring disputes among the shareholders or between them and the Company, to "arbiters in France for judgment and with appeals before the Imperial Court of Paris as being a superarbiter."

In view of France's widely accepted claim to have brought civilization to backward peoples and to stand for the liberty of the individual, it is of interest to note that the first article of the agreement sponsored by Turkey in 1866, is entitled "Abolition of Forced Labor from the Canal Works." Egypt then agreed to pay an indemnity of 38 million francs to the Suez Canal Company, in order to cancel the 1856 concession given to De Lesseps to use impressed Egyptian laborers on the construction of the Canal—a concession which had caused the death of many thousands of Egyptians for the benefit of French and British shareholders.

In return for Egypt's payment of 38 million francs as compensation for annulment of the right of the French-directed Suez Canal Company to use forced labor, the latter graciously agreed henceforth to "employ the necessary workmen for the enterprise according to common law."

In this and the previous agreements of 1854 and 1856 between Egypt and the Suez Canal Company, it was made clear that the Canal, and the lands adjacent leased to the Suez Canal Company, for the construction of installations necessary for the Canal's operation, remained part of the Egyptian domain. They remained under the authority of the Egyptian police, and the Government of Egypt reserved the right to occupy "any position or strategic point it judges necessary for the defense of the country."

There can therefore be no doubt, as John T. Flynn pointed out in his broadcasts over the Mutual Network, that President Nasser of Egypt was exercising the same right of "eminent domain" when he nationalized the Suez Canal, as President Roosevelt when he established the Tennessee Valley Authority.

"The Porte," meaning the Turkish Government, as overlord of Egypt, refused, on January 10, 1872, to agree to proposals for an international organization to run the Canal, saying that it "could not admit, even in principle, the sale of the Canal, or the creation of an International Administration on its own territory."

The Constantinople Convention, signed on October 29, 1888, by Great Britain, Germany, Austria, Hungary, Spain, France, Italy, the Netherlands and Turkey, made Egypt, not the Suez Canal Company, the guarantor of unhampered traffic through whatever agency she might designate to control the Canal.

The Convention specifically states, in Article XII, that "the rights of Turkey as the territorial power are reserved," thus preserving Egypt's right of "eminent domain." Nor did the Convention make any provision for the sanctity of the concession made to the Suez Canal Company. On the contrary, Article XIV expressly provides that the provisions of the Convention should operate independently of the concession to the Suez Canal Company. Thus there is no connection between the two, although the American public has been misled into identifying them.

As Mr. Robert Delson, an expert on international law, wrote in the June 27 issue of the *Reporter:*

> The view of the Canal Company as the convention-bred, internationally appointed and privileged guardian angel of free passage runs aground on the terms of the convention itself, which provided that everybody ought to be able to go back and forth through the Canal, *not that everybody ought to own and operate it.* [Italics added.]

As Mr. Delson points out, there is no basis in the text of the Convention to justify the 1956 statement made by British Foreign Secretary Selwyn Lloyd that operation by the Suez Canal Company "formed part of the basis of the Convention." Nor that of Mr. Dulles when he said that the 1866 concession to the Suez Canal Company "has been by reference incorporated into and made part of what is called the definitive system set up by the 1888 treaty . . . establishing the rights of the . . . company." Mr. Dulles was evidently in too much of a hurry to study the text, and was misled by his experts, when he said that "the operating rights and assets of the company were impressed with an international interest" by the Constantinople Convention. For this treaty, far from incorporating or guaranteeing Egypt's concession to the Suez Canal Company, was designed to "transform a discretionary right exercised by Egypt under a private arrangement (with the Suez Canal Company) into a legal obligation imposed by treaty."

Whichever way it is interpreted, the Constantinople Convention has been honored more in the breach than in the observance, thanks to the contradictory provisions of its various articles, to Britain's refusal for more than two decades to ratify its main articles, and to the unilateral abrogation by Britain and France in 1904 of its most important clause guaranteeing the free passage of the ships of all nations even in time of war.

But in one respect its terms are clear enough to justify Egypt's contention that she has the right to refuse to allow Israeli ships to pass through the Suez Canal, so long as there is only an armistice between her and the State of Israel. For in Article X it is written that the provisions concerning free passage of the Canal "even to ships of war of belligerents" shall not interefere with measures which Egypt or her suzerain (at that time the Sultan of Turkey) "might find it necessary to take securing by their own forces the defense of Egypt and the maintenance of public order."

This same Article X also states that the provisions of Articles IV, V, VII and VIII of the treaty shall "in no case occasion any obstacle to the measures which the Imperial Ottoman Government may think it necessary to take in order to insure by its own forces the defence of its other possessions situated on the eastern coast of the Red Sea."

Britain, after her army had occupied Egypt in 1884, maintained the same opposition to the internationalization of the Suez Canal as Turkey before her. At a conference held in Paris in June 1885, the British representative, Mr. Pauncefote, in indicating his Government's approval of the Convention (subsequently signed in Constantinople in 1888), made the reservation that this "did not limit the freedom of action of England so long as she was in occupation of Egypt." And Lord Salisbury (whose descendant was to resign from the British Cabinet in 1957 in protest at Prime Minister Macmillan's enforced recognition of Egypt's right to run the Canal), sent a circular to the Powers in 1887 reserving England's freedom of action in Egypt irrespective of the terms of the Constantinople Convention. Eleven years later, on July 12, 1898, Mr. Curzon, then British Under Secretary of State for Foreign Affairs, replied to a question in the House of Commons as to whether the Constantinople Convention was in force by saying:

> It was certainly in existence . . . but has not been brought into practical operation. This is owing to the reserve made on behalf of H.M.'s Government by the British delegates to the Suez Canal Commission in 1885, which were reserved by Lord Salisbury, and communicated to the Powers in 1887.

Britain continued for nearly two decades in her refusal to permit the clauses of the Constantinople Convention guaranteeing free passage through the Canal at all times to the ships of all nations to go into effect. When she finally did so, in 1904 (as part of her bargain with France to give the latter a free hand in Morocco in return for a free hand for Britain in Egypt) the British Government made a reservation which annulled, or indefinitely held in abeyance, its most important provision, namely, the last sentence of paragraph I, which reads: "The Canal shall never be subjected to the exercise of the right of blockade."

In 1922, when the British granted nominal independence to Egypt, they reserved exclusive power to control and defend the Canal. Today, when Egypt is held guilty of treaty breaking on account of her refusal to permit Israeli ships to pass through the Canal, we should take note of the precedent set by England when she ruled over Egypt and expressly refused to commit herself or her Egyptian vassal to the non-exercise of belligerent rights.

Without any audible protest from any of the signatories of the Constantinople Convention, except Germany, Austria and maybe Turkey during the 1914 war, and Italy as well as Germany during World War II, Britain kept the Canal open only for Allied ships.

I am indebted to Mr. Delson's article in the *Reporter* for knowledge of another interesting fact which I had not known. He writes that when Rommel was only fifty miles from the Canal in 1943, "President Roosevelt sought assurances that Britain was prepared to blow up the Canal if necessary—despite the provision of the Convention that the Canal was to remain open in time of war as well as in peace."

While exercising her "protectorate" over Egypt, Britain was as emphatic in asserting that the Suez Canal Company was an Egyptian company, as in maintaining the contrary thesis in 1956.

For instance, in 1939, in a memorandum submitted to the Mixed Courts in Egypt which pronounced judgment in its favor in February 1940, the British Government maintained:

> The Suez Canal Company is a legal person in accordance with Egyptian law. Its nationality and character are solely Egyptian. It is, therefore, subject to Egyptian laws.
>
> It is true that the Company is given the name "The Universal Company of the Maritime Suez Canal." . . . this designation cannot deprive the Company of its Egyptian nationality. *The Company is Egyptian in accordance with the established general principles of law* and in particular with the principles of private international laws and the Company's organic law.
>
> It is Egyptian because it is granted a concession which

> has for its object Egyptian private assets and because its principal center is in Egypt.
>
> And because it cannot be Egyptian and non-Egyptian at the same time. This would be a legal anomaly . . . and contradictory to the general principles of law. [Italics added.]

Lastly, it should be noted that Article VIII of the agreement concluded between Egypt and Britain in 1954 states specifically that the Suez Canal is an integral part of Egypt.

In the 1954 Anglo-Egyptian Treaty relinquishing British sovereignty over Egypt there is no mention of the Suez Canal Company; and the only reference to the Constantinople Convention to be found in this document is an affirmation to "uphold the 1888 Convention guaranteeing freedom of navigation of the Canal."

Britain, obviously, could not demand that Egypt should undertake to interpret or observe the provisions of this Convention in a different manner to His Majesty's Government.

In 1914, when Britain barred the Suez Canal to German and Austrian shipping, Egypt was nominally a part of Turkey, which was still neutral, so that the articles of the Constantinople Convention, which exempted Egypt from the obligation to allow free passage for the ships of all nations in time of war and peace, when necessary in her own self-defense, were legally inapplicable. Nevertheless, when on August 18, 1914, an Austrian merchant ship, the "Carcadero," which was unequipped with wireless, and whose master was consequently unaware of the outbreak of war, arrived unsuspectingly at Suez, British forces seized her and she was condemned as a prize.

As Mr. Delson remarks, "The Convention signers and current champions turned their back on the principles when it suited them to do so."

If Egypt is held guilty of violating international law and the Constantinople Convention by barring Israeli ships from the

Suez Canal, then the United States must be held similarly culpable with regard to the Panama Canal. For the neutralization provisions of the Hay-Pauncefote Treaty of 1901 (to which the United States had to agree in order to rid herself of an obligation not to construct the Canal except in conjunction with England) are modelled on the Constantinople Convention of 1888, which Sir Julian Pauncefote had himself also negotiated, in Paris in 1885. Nevertheless, shortly after the United States entered World War I, President Wilson issued a proclamation forbidding the use of the Panama Canal to German and Austrian ships. Moreover, this proclamation remained in effect after the United States, together with her allies, had signed an armistice with Germany at Compiègne on November 11, 1918, and even after the signing of a peace treaty with Germany at Versailles in June 1919. Because the Versailles treaty was debated for many months in the Senate and finally rejected, peace was not made between the United States and Germany until the Treaty of Berlin on August 25, 1921. During this whole three-year period of "armistice" the Canal remained closed to German shipping (except, if one can call it an exception, those German ships which had been seized by the Allied Powers).

In view of these precedents it is impossible to maintain the thesis that Egypt in barring the Suez Canal to ships of the State of Israel during a state of armistice is contravening the Constantinople Convention or international law. Moreover, Israeli ships had not been permitted to pass the Suez Canal before the British withdrew from Egypt, so that the nationalization decree had nothing whatever to do with the issue.

Nor can Nasser on other counts be accused of having contravened the Constantinople Convention of 1888, since Egypt, after nationalizing the Suez Canal Company, managed to keep the Canal in full operation in spite of the endeavors made by the French directors of the Company to sabotage its operations.

It was France and England, not Egypt, which in 1956 endeavored to interrupt free passage through the Canal, when the directors of the Suez Canal Company offered their pilots a two-year salary bonus, and threatened those who stayed with loss of their pensions, to induce them to quit working. M. Georges-Picot, the Director General of the Suez Canal Company (as well as a French representative in the United Nations) stated on August 6 that nearly all the non-Egyptian pilots were "loyal" and said, "I could tomorrow end all traffic on the Canal if I chose to give the order for repatriation. The Company is now in a position to use the loyalty of its employees to paralyze the Canal at any time it chooses." Thus, when on September 11 the pilots pulled out, London and Paris were confident that they had placed Nasser on the horns of an insoluble dilemma. In the words of the *London Times* correspondent in Paris: "Either shipping will be held up or the Egyptians will force the employees to remain, and it is felt here that either event could well provide Britain and France with a pretext for military intervention." A different pretext had to be contrived when Egypt managed to keep as large convoys as before moving through the Suez Canal and also permitted passage even to the British and French ships which refused to pay dues to Egypt. It was not Egypt but England and France, who in collaboration with Israel eventually caused the blockade of the Suez Canal by their aggression against Egypt.

Egypt's success was due mainly to the endurance and patriotism of the Egyptian pilots who worked round the clock; to the Greeks, whose support in this time of crisis was gratefully acknowledged by Nasser; and to the loyal service of some pilots of other nationalities who refused to be tempted by the large sums offered them to quit working. Also German pilots from the Kiel Canal came to Egypt to offer their services, in spite of the sudden increase in their salaries announced by Dr. Adenauer's government, which, in pursuance of its policy of conciliating France, endeavored to prevent any assistance being given to Egypt. Nasser was also helped in his successful endeavor to keep the Canal open by American, Italian and Scandinavian volunteers who responded to his appeal for pilots to replace those withdrawn by France in her efforts to sabotage the working of the Suez Canal. Also some Russian and Yugoslav pilots were ordered to Egypt by their governments.

All in all, the success of the Egyptian Government in keeping the Canal operating afforded proof that Egypt could stand on her own feet without help from Britain and France, and win in spite of Anglo-French efforts to sabotage the operations of the Canal. I was also told in Egypt that the new German pilots with typical efficiency had offered advice enabling the new Egyptian management to shorten by two hours the time formerly required for convoys to pass through the Canal.

Either by reason of their lack of knowledge, or because their editorial writers and pundits were too angry to study the evidence and the historical record, many American newspapers, in particular the *New York Times,* continued falsely to accuse Egypt of being a violator of treaties and international law, and of having thus "provoked" the Anglo-French attack.

Ignorance, or belief in things which "just ain't so," can be as harmful as a big lie, since if untrue statements are reiterated often enough in the press and over the radio they come to be believed and lead to a perversion of policy.

Whether President Nasser was wise, even though legally justified, in prematurely abrogating the concession given to the Suez Canal Company which would have expired in 1968, is a different question. Had he not lost his temper and let his desire to make America "choke on her own fury" drive him to precipitate action, he could have got what he wanted with comparatively slight opposition, and would not have undermined the influence of his Western friends or lost their support. For it was not so much what he did as the way he did it which affronted public opinion in America and England.

If the Egyptian Government had followed acceptable Western procedures for the nationalization of private enterprise, the world would have known what it never learned—namely, the valid grounds for the decision in 1956 to cancel the Suez Canal Company's concession which was due to expire in 1968. Had Nasser and his advisers not lacked knowledge of the art of public relations, or had they not themselves been blinded by their fury, they would have proceeded along some such lines as the following:

First there could have been appointed a commission of lawyers, engineers and other experts to study the problem of modernizing the Canal to accommodate the large tankers being constructed by the oil companies. This commission would naturally have recommended that the Canal be deepened and widened to make it possible for the new "super tankers" to pass. The Suez Canal Company would then have been put on the spot. If it agreed to invest the huge sums necessary for the widening and deepening of the Canal, it would never be able to reimburse itself by tolls collected from the big new tankers, since its concession was due to expire in 1968. If it refused, Egypt would have been justified in exercising her right of "eminent domain" to nationalize the Canal Company, in order to promote not only her own interests but those of the "users" of the Canal.

By adopting some such procedure as this, Egypt would not only have placed the Suez Canal Company in an unfavorable light, but also have enlisted the "users" of the Canal on her side. She could also have embarrassed England by proposing that the millions of pounds of Egyptian sterling credits, created by Egyptian loans to Britain during World War II, which Egypt was permitted to realize only little by little, be applied to the transfer to Egypt of Britain's holdings in the Suez Canal Company. If Britain agreed to such a transfer of stock, Egypt would have dominated the Suez Canal Company. If she refused, Britain would have seemed to be a dog in the manger, and Egypt's nationalization decree would have been regarded in a more favorable light.

In addition to the case which Egypt could have made out of the failure of the Suez Canal Company to utilize part of its revenue to widen and deepen the Canal to meet modern requirements, she had other just causes for complaint, as well as valid economic reasons which if advanced would have made her nationalization decree less clumsy.

The Canal tolls, which in 1955 amounted to approximately 100 million dollars, had shown an ever-increasing revenue, but Egypt was reaping little benefit. The Canal carried three times as much traffic as the Panama Canal. Nasser, if he economized on all government expenditures and if he could obtain aid from the Soviet Government or other sources, might have been enabled to construct his High Dam out of Canal revenue and still leave enough over to compensate the shareholders and keep the Canal in working order. He knew that a large proportion of the revenues collected by the Suez Canal Company was being dissipated by the fantastically high sums paid to its directors in Paris, some of whom were receiving $100,000 a year for their "services," which, valuable as they might be in increasing the assets of the Company by speculation or investment in other fields, were of little or no value to Egypt. Egypt also had abundant grounds for the supposition that, in anticipation of the coming end of its concession, the Suez Canal Company was neglecting its obligations concerning the normal repairs and upkeep of the Canal.

According to the Egyptian Government's indictment, which seems never to have been refuted by the Directors of the Suez Canal Company, it had failed to carry out the following commitments:

The conversion of Lake Timsah into an inland harbor capable of receiving vessels of the highest tonnage as provided for in the Act of Concession.

To keep Port Said harbor, which it administrated, in a suitable condition to meet the requirements of transit trade. "Despite the commercial importance of this harbor," the Egyptian Government states in its White Paper on the Nationalization of the Suez Canal Company, "it lacks quays for the landing of vessels," so that "loading and unloading are still carried on in the open sea by old fashioned methods which contribute to the high cost of commerce, transit trade in particular."

Certainly the Egyptian Government had cause to complain that the Suez Canal Company was not utilizing a sufficient share of its increasing revenues to enlarge its carrying capacity or to improve and modernize its harbors and installations. Instead it was paying absurdly high salaries to its directors in Paris and using the Canal's profits for investments outside Egypt to increase the assets abroad whose ownership is now in dispute between Egypt, France and Britain. The Egyptian Government was also concerned with the failure of the Suez Canal Company to train Egyptian pilots to take the place of the foreign ones who were being retired or were due for retirement with pensions soon after the expiration of the concession to the Suez Canal Company.

In a word, Egypt had a very good case against the Suez Canal Company which justified the nationalization decree, but failed to present it to the world, owing to Nasser's angry and thoughtless reaction to the insult and injury he sustained when in July 1956 the United States Administration withdrew its offer to help finance construction of the Aswan High Dam.

The previous December the United States had offered to give 54.6 million dollars toward the 400 million of foreign exchange required for this 1.2 billion dollar project; and to consider sympathetically future aid which would have brought the the American and British total contribution to 200 million dollars spread over ten to fifteen years with America supplying 75 percent. The International Bank for Reconstruction and Development promised to loan 200 million dollars and Egypt herself undertook to provide the remainder of the cost in the form of service and material. At this point it seemed that Russia's sale of arms to Egypt had galvanized the West to offer to finance this gigantic project which would increase the cultivatable area of overpopulated Egypt by 25 per cent and supply electric power for her industrial development. Substantial aid was to be given to the country which had hitherto received far less than her "fair share" of foreign aid, although her need was so much greater than that of other countries far more generously aided by the United States. Egypt, which had received only 34 million dollars out of a total of 53 billions of grants and credits given to foreign countries up to the end of 1955, could well claim to have been slighted. Nasser had previously offered objections to some of the requirements of the World Bank for the loan, and he now endeavored to secure more favorable terms by hinting that Russia had made him an offer of a loan of 300 million dollars for the project with no strings attached.

In thus attempting to exert pressure on the United States, Nasser made a bad blunder, or was at least very unlucky. His use of the method hitherto effectively employed by other countries came at a moment when the United States Administration had decided that it was losing friends and alienating allies by being nicer to neutrals, and that it was time to call Russia's hand by making an example of Egypt. He can hardly be blamed for his costly miscalculation in view of America's previous record of giving aid more generously, or with fewer strings attached, to "uncommitted" nations or to such friends of our enemies as Yugoslavia and India, than to those committed to our side—with the exception, of course, of our old allies, France and England. In 1956 the United States was giving more than a third of the total of its economic aid to the uncommitted nations or to those who were neutral against us. Nasser himself had been offered financial aid for the building of his High Dam only after he had entered into trade relations with the Soviet Empire by bartering Egypt's cotton for Czechoslovak arms. He had also, no doubt, taken note of the fact that the first Western reaction to his arms deal with the Soviet Empire had been a futile appeal by Macmillan, Pinay and Dulles to Molotov (in September 1955 in New York) to preserve "the spirit of Geneva" by stopping the shipment of Czech arms to Egypt. Since the Western Powers were so ready to make a deal with Moscow at his expense, it was hardly surprising that Nasser reacted by telling America that he too could act in accordance with the spirit of Geneva by making his own bargain with the Kremlin.

Whether or not Nasser was so foolish as to believe that Soviet Russia was capable of competing economically with the United States by giving Egypt a huge loan, the United States Administration knew better and took the opportunity to call the Soviet bluff. Hence, apparently, the brusque withdrawal of America's ten-month-old offer to help finance the construction of the Aswan Dam, when the Egyptian Ambassador to the United States called on the State Department in July 1956 to accept the offer on our terms.

This, at least, is the only plausible explanation which has been offered for the rude rebuff to Egypt which led to Nasser's nationalization of the Suez Canal and the Suez War. While this interpretation, given in *Time* magazine's John R. Beal's semi-authorized biography of John Foster Dulles published in 1957, provoked a denial by Dulles, Mr. Beale's account of what happened and why it happened appears substantially correct. Answering the question, "Why did Dulles turn down Nasser so brutally, without a chance to save face?" Beale writes:

> As a calculated risk his decision was on a grand scale. . . . It risked opening a key Middle East country whose territory bracketed the strategic Suez Canal, to communist economic and political penetration. It risked alienating other Arab nations, controlling an oil supply without which Western Europe's mechanized industry and military defenses would be defenseless.
>
> Dulles' bet was placed on the belief that it would expose the shallow character of Russia's foreign economic pretensions. . . ."

If, in spite of Mr. Dulles' diplomatic denials this is the correct explanation, one wonders why he chose Egypt, instead of Yugoslavia, or Ceylon, or Indonesia, or Nehru's India—all of which were far more friendly to the Moscow-Peking axis than Nasser's Egypt?

In view of the Eisenhower-Dulles record in the conduct of American foreign policy, before as well as during the Suez crisis, it is unlikely that Zionist or Anglo-French pressures caused the Secretary of State to choose Egypt to make an example of the perils of flirtations with Soviet Russia. It would rather seem that Mr. Dulles, in his preoccupation with America's worldwide struggle against Communist tyranny, failed to realize the consequences of picking on Egypt to prove that America is not to be influenced by blackmail. But whatever motivated the Secretary of State, the fact remains that by suddenly withdrawing America's offer to help finance the construction of the Aswan Dam, the State Department placed Nasser's government in an intolerable position and caused it to react in a manner which immensely benefited Soviet Russia. The reason given by the State Department—namely, that the condition of the Egyptian economy did not justify the loan—seemed a gratuitous insult.

The subcommittee of the Senate Armed Services and Foreign Relations Committees, appointed in January 1957 to review our Middle East policy since 1946 with a view to ascertaining how and why the Suez crisis had arisen, failed to issue a report. The reason given was that the State Department had not provided the subcommittee with a white paper, or chronological statement with supporting documents, and because the volume of papers, measuring more than a foot high on the subject of the Aswan Dam alone, was not only indigestible but consisted for the most part of secret or top secret documents. However, Senator Fulbright, the chairman of the subcommittee, took time out to discover the facts buried in the huge pile, and on August 14 told the Senate that on the basis of the evidence, which he was precluded from quoting on account of its being classified, he had come to the following conclusion:

> The Aswan Dam project was a sound project from the point of view of engineering feasibility and it was a reasonable risk for economic development loans. Sources of capital other than those involved in the offer which was made to Egypt, both private sources and other government sources, were definitely interested in pursuing the project.
>
> . . . it was recognized that the Aswan Dam . . . was vital to the future of Egypt . . . without such a development, Egypt with its increasing population, may be expected to suffer a constantly lowering standard of living . . . [causing] social and political unrest in Egypt . . . [and endangering] the unstable peace of the Middle East.

> The Administration's decision to withdraw the offer to Egypt was made against the advice of the United States Ambassador to Egypt, and the President of the International Bank for Reconstruction and Development.

Mr. Dulles' stated reasons for the withdrawal of the offer were demolished by Senator Fulbright one by one.

The major drain on Egypt's resources, payment for Czech arms, had occurred prior to the time of the United States offer to help finance the Aswan Dam. It therefore could not justify the withdrawal of the offer seven months later. On the contrary, as he remarked in the course of his argument with Senator Knowland in the Senate, "the arms deal was one of the principal reasons which motivated our government and the British, and was the principal reason for the offer being made." There was, he continued, no evidence of any radical worsening of Egypt's economic position, and the American Chairman of the International Bank, which would have contributed a 200 million dollar loan, was still in favor of the project. Nor was there any evidence that the Sudan or other "Nile riparian states" would have refused their consent to the construction of the Aswan Dam, since they too would have derived substantial benefits.

As regards Mr. Dulles' final argument, that "congressional opposition" was a factor causing the withdrawal of United States financial aid to Egypt, Senator Fulbright was on less sure ground. Since he failed even to mention Israel, and had nothing to say concerning the Truman Administration's responsibility for the Middle East muddle by reason of its sponsorship of the United Nations partition of Palestine, he can be accused of playing politics by concentrating his fire on the Republican Administration's Egyptian blunders. However, the Arkansas Senator must, at least, be given credit for having admitted that the Senators from the cotton-growing states, one of which he himself represents, were opposed to the construction of the

Aswan Dam, which they feared would mean increased competition from Egypt. In his view, their fears were "insubstantial"; but he also said that their interests should not, in any case, be permitted to stand in the way of a project of benefit to the United States as a whole. Moreover, he was of the opinion that their objections could have been overcome if the overriding argument of American interest had been presented to them by the State Department.

Construction of the Aswan Dam with United States financial backing would have provided the whole of the Middle East with such "a dramatic example of the West's ability and willingness to undertake major developments for the improvement of the standard of living, that it would have been of great importance in the settlement of the differences, political and social, in that area."

More important still was Senator Fulbright's perception that Dulles "confused Egyptian nationalism and neutralism with communism," thus delaying "the day when the Egyptian people might seek to build a democratic government on a solid economic basis." If we had helped Egypt concentrate on internal development instead of foreign adventures, we could have helped "to create stability throughout the Middle East." In Senator Fulbright's words:

> Despite the judgment of able State Department career officials indicating that Nasser had some appreciation of the dangers of dealing too closely with the Soviet Union, Mr. Dulles seemed to believe that Nasser had become a Soviet puppet. He did not recognize that Egyptian nationalism was a powerful force which could, if recognized for what it was and carefully handled, be directed toward political freedom instead of communism. . . . He also failed to appreciate the tremendous emotional importance which all Egyptians attached to the building of the dam. He did

not appreciate the effect the building of the dam would have had upon the entire Arab world as an example of our willingness to help them help themselves.

As subsequent events have proved, Senator Fulbright was also right when he said that the withdrawal of the offer to help finance the Aswan Dam led to the Suez War,* and enabled the Soviet to place "a hammer lock on a country which otherwise might well have stayed relatively free from influence by the Soviet orbit."

Undoubtedly, a more farsighted, rational and diplomatic handling of American interests in the Middle East could have prevented our relationship with Egypt from deteriorating to the point that "Nasser was prompted to abandon the possibility of friendship with us, and to turn instead to the only large nation still proferring what must have seemed to him to be a hand of friendship."

These words, from Senator Fulbright's speech to the Senate on August 14, 1957, express a view of the situation in the Middle East crisis so similar to my own that I have inserted them in my text at the moment of going to press. The fact that I have differed from his views, and those of other eminent Democratic and Republican liberals on other issues, notably as regards China, is of less importance than our present common recognition of the basic realities in the dangerously explosive situation in the Middle East. How those fundamental principles which

* America's proposed contribution to the cost of construction of the Dam—15 million dollars a year for ten years—was chicken feed as compared with the billion we gave France for her futile war in Indochina; or to the hundreds of millions we have given to the Yugoslav and Polish Communist Governments over the past decade. Moreover, we have already expended 174 million dollars in 1957 in the Middle East under the Eisenhower Doctrine in our attempt to annul the advantages gained by Moscow by the Suez War.

made America great and free and strong can be applied in a changing world is a matter of debate. But knowledge of the facts is the prerequisite of any intelligent discussion, whatever the motives of those who reveal them. And the evidence, as presented by Senator Fulbright, gives substance to the argument that John Foster Dulles is as guilty as Gamal Nasser of having been influenced more by emotion, or by immediate political considerations, than by hard-headed realism in the pursuit of vital national objectives. One thing is certain: the Secretary of State displayed a fatal lack of understanding of the susceptibilities of newly emancipated nations when he not only deprived Egypt of the hope of freedom from starvation by means of American assistance in constructing the Aswan Dam, but added insult to injury by telling her that she was unworthy of our aid.

Dulles not only shattered Nasser's dream of securing American financial aid in solving, or alleviating, Egypt's desperate problem of overpopulation and increasing poverty, intensified by the ever-diminishing demand for her cotton in America and England, thus impelling him to attempt to get the means to construct his Dam by nationalizing the Suez Canal Company. The United States rebuff was also taken to mean that the United States had reversed its former policy of supporting Nasser's reformist and progressive regime. Having lost America's backing, it seemed doomed to destruction from its enemies at home and abroad unless it could secure Soviet backing, or unless it could at least prevent the threatened alliance of right and left-wing Egyptian extremists against it by means of an understanding with Moscow.

Nasser's land reform had alienated the Egyptian landowners who had waxed fat on the misery of the Egyptian *fellahin.* This and other reforms aiming at a new deal for the Egyptian peasants and workers, together with the institution of a cleaner and better government than Egypt had known for hundreds of years, had secured him the support of the majority of the population and given him popularity and influence all over the Arab world. But he had likewise incurred the hostility of both Egyptian and foreign vested interests in the polygot business community of Cairo and Alexandria. His opposition to the fanatics of the Moslem League, as also to the Communists and their dupes who were dissatisfied with his gradual reforms, had made him still more enemies. In a word, Nasser's attempt to steer Egypt along a course enabling her to progress along Western democratic lines was beset with dangers from both the right and the left, and now it seemed that he had lost his American pilot.

A United States Secretary of State whose global view took far too little account of the needs, necesssities, feelings and aspirations of any of the pawns in the chess game between the United States and the USSR had played into Russia's hand by his rebuff to Egypt. No pawn likes to be regarded as expendable, or to have his dignity and worth denied. Each one of them dreams of reaching the end of the board and becoming a queen, bishop, castle or knight. The United States which is so careful of the feelings of its favored allies in Europe, and of such neutrals as Nehru, has displayed a singular lack of regard for the dignity and susceptibilities of the Arabs. We have continued to play idiot's chess, by labelling Egypt a pawn of no potentiality and by willfully sacrificing her as a horrible example to other ambitious pawns who might wish to play a stronger role in the deadly game between the free world and Communism.

In my notes of my interview with Nasser, as in his speeches, and those of other Arab leaders, the words "national dignity" recurred again and again. Peoples who have smarted under the indignities they have suffered under Western domination, irrespective of whether alien rule improved or worsened their material condition, are acutely sensitive to affronts to their dignity or self-respect and national pride. Americans who have for so long enjoyed the independence and liberty their forefathers fought and died to win, who have no experience or memory of being treated as inferiors, and who have never even suffered from the class distinctions which still cause heartache and bitterness in Europe, are naturally inclined to disregard, or fail to understand, the sensitivity of less fortunate peoples still smarting under the slights and humiliation endured under the rule of foreign conquerors, or occupation forces.

"The refusal to treat Egypt as an equal" was the main objection raised to the Dulles plan to set up a Suez canal users' association by the Middle East Research Center in Cairo, which denounced it as "conceived as a closed body with a definite membership, set apart from the scores of other countries using the Canal."

Perhaps if Mr. Dulles had had greater appreciation of the lingering resentment of African and Asiatic peoples toward the Europeans who formerly humiliated them by treating them as an inferior race, he would not have picked on Egypt as the country to punish for its dealings with Moscow, while he continued to support the Communist dictator of Yugoslavia.

When asked by *Look* correspondent William Attwood, in the interview published in its June 25, 1957, issue, why he had not waited until 1969, when the Canal would automatically have reverted to Egypt, Nasser replied:

> For two reasons. When you said you would not help us to build the High Dam, we had to show you that you cannot insult a small country and get away with it. If we had accepted the slap in the face, you would have slapped us again. Also we needed to raise money to build the dam ourselves. The Canal tolls were a logical source of income.

. . . We were studying the question of nationalizing the Canal, but had not reached a decision. You made up our minds for us.

The Egyptians are particularly sensitive to affronts by the West on account of the wrongs and indignities inflicted upon them by the British during most of the period of their eighty-year occupation. As the British Labor M.P. Michael Foot has said: "The Egypt of 1956 with all its poverty and prickly nationalism was made in England."

The British occupation, which was supposed to be only "temporary," began in 1882 when Prime Minister Gladstone sent warships to bombard Alexandria, and landed 25,000 British troops in order to destroy Ahmed Arabi Bey, the Egyptian nationalist leader of that time who sought to end the corrupt and oppressive regime of the spendthrift Khedives ruling in the name of the Turkish Sultan. Arabi, who pinned his faith on Gladstone's liberal professions and desired friendship with England, was defeated and put on trial for his life, and his country returned to its oppressors. As Michael Foot and Mervyn Jones say in their book, *Guilty Men* (New York: Rinehart, 1957), "The gentle Arabi was the 1882 model of an Egyptian nationalist, not the toughened, embittered type of 1956 . . . and was no match for British Imperialism [which used] the 'resources of civilisation,' lying, treachery and fraud." It is of interest to note that Arabi refused to follow the advice of his strategic advisers to blockade the Suez Canal as soon as Britain attacked.

Winston Churchill, who three quarters of a century later was to oppose the British withdrawal from Egypt, and to favor the attack on Suez to destroy Nasser and reestablish British imperial rights, records in his life of his father that Lord Randolph Churchill sympathized with Arabi's revolt and subscribed £50 to the expense of the Egyptian's defense before a court martial, because Lord Churchill believed Arabi to be "the head of a real national movement directed against one of the vilest and most worthless governments in the world."

To Sir Winston Churchill's father, England's use of her power to stamp out Arabi's movement and hand back the Egyptians to the Khedive, and to the extortions of his creditors, was "an odious crime" and the war on Egypt "a wicked and unjust bondholders war." Three quarters of a century later the son backed Eden in just such another war on Egypt.

During the ensuing years, up to and after World War II, indignities as well as injuries were inflicted on those whom their British overlords contemptuously referred to as "Wogs," and to whom they brought few of the benefits which British colonial rule brought to other lands. Britain, while exploiting Egypt for the benefit of "the bondholders," maintained the corrupt and inequitable social and economic structure inherited from the Turks which had made of Egypt a country in which a ruling class of wealthy Pashas owned almost all the land, and where the cultivators became progressively poorer with the increase in population and the failure substantially to increase the irrigated land by public works. When the Egyptian Nationalists ousted King Farouk and started their land reform, less than two thousand landowners owned a quarter of the cultivatable land, while another three or four thousand owned another quarter. This in a country where fourteen out of twenty million strive to get a living from the land and where, according to a 1952 United Nations report, the amount of cultivatable land per head of the population was only a quarter of an acre, making Egypt the most overpopulated country in the world. Yet it is Nasser, not the British, who is usually held responsible for the semi-starved condition of the Egyptian *fellahin,* whose misery he had hoped to alleviate by construction of the High Dam at Aswan.

All in all, the facts bear out the contention of such Left Wing British writers as Michael Foot and Mervyn Jones, in their book entitled *Guilty Men,* in which they admit that in England's dealings with some other nations "liberal Britain has fulfilled its nobler aspirations," but add, "Second only to Ireland, our story in Egypt is one of deceit and shame and of brute force failing to achieve its brutal ends."

Even if British rule had brought material benefits instead of increasing poverty for the mass of the population, the personal humiliations inflicted on the Egyptians would nevertheless have produced the sensitivity and suspicion of "the West" which give Nasser his mass support when he defies us. As a British contributor to the conservative British weekly, the *Spectator,* wrote in the December 28, 1956 issue:

> During the Second World War, no leadership from the Residency in Cairo restrained the racial conceit and zoological xenophobia of the hundreds of thousands of the British bearers of the white man's burden, both commissioned and non-commissioned, which ran amok in the Middle East in the Forties. . . .
>
> No gesture was made to underline at least some community of aims and ideals with Egypt when the war against Germany was won. . .
>
> [Egypt was] evacuated a couple of years later under circumstances which convinced the Egyptian leaders that the British, for all their fine talk about human rights and democracy, respond only to a kick in the teeth, preferably a strong one.

The lesson learnt by Egypt from the West—namely that only force counts—was reinforced when Winston Churchill, reluctantly agreeing in July 1954 to the withdrawal of British forces from Egypt, said he was doing so only because the hydrogen bomb had convinced him that the Suez base was obsolete. Thus

Britain herself laid the groundwork for the Egyptian supposition, powerfully substantiated durng the Suez War, that liberation from British occupation and defense against British attack, were due to Russia and her possession of the atomic bomb. "The West" itself taught Colonel Nasser that England respects force far more than the liberal principles she teaches but too often ignores.

It would be tedious to recount all the backing and filling, negotiations, claims and counter-claims which preceded the Suez War. But if one studies the record it seems clear that the British and French governments wanted a showdown instead of a peaceful settlement.

In September when Sir Anthony Eden mistakenly understood that Dulles was agreed that the "Users Association" would, if necessary, shoot its way through the Canal, the Tories in Parliament exulted that they were going back to Suez with America behind them. This dream was shattered when President Eisenhower made a trans-Atlantic call to Eden, and Dulles told a Washington press conference that he knew nothing about any plan to take over the Canal by force. Subsequently Egypt agreed to the six points proposed by the United Nations as the basis for negotiating a settlement, and it was precisely then that England and France attacked her.

As the London *Economist,* whose reports on the Suez crisis were particularly well informed and objective, said on May 18, 1957:

> British and French policy after the seizure of the Canal suffered from the fundamental defect that its underlying intention was not to negotiate a Canal settlement but to bring about the downfall of Colonel Nasser.

After Britain and France launched their attack, broadcasts to Egypt left no doubt that Nasser's overthrow was the primary war aim. As quoted in the House of Commons on November 5 by Sir Wedgewood Benn, a broadcast to Egypt from Cyprus early that morning had said:

> It means that we are obliged to bomb you wherever you are. Imagine your villages being bombed. Imagine your wives, children, mothers, fathers and grandfathers escaping from their houses and leaving their property behind. This will happen to you if you hide behind your women in the villages. . . . If they do not evacuate, there is no doubt that your villages and homes will be destroyed. You have committed a sin . . . that is, you placed your confidence in Abdul Nasser.

Another M.P. quoted from a leaflet dropped over Egypt by the R.A.F. which according to the B.B.C., said, "We have the might and we shall use it to the limit if you do not give in."

As Aneurin Bevan said in the debate which followed, "We have here, not a military action to separate Egypt and Israeli troops, but a declaration of war against the Egyptian Government in the most brutal terms."

Another leaflet said:

> Your choice is clear. Either accept the Allied proposals, which will bring you peace with honour and prosperity, or accept the consequences of Nasser's policy, which will bring heavy retribution not only to the few who are guilty but also to you—the many—who are innocent.

A later broadcast, following the British landing at Port Said said:

> Very soon it will be dark. Soldiers in Port Said, you are in a hopeless situation. Protect your lives. It is not your duty to die for your country. You have seen the Commandos

> fight by day. Have you ever seen them fight by night? The first thing you will know is when you feel cold steel in your back.

According to British reports, although there had been tough fighting at the airfield, resistance in the city came mainly from snipers and ill-armed civilian levies in the Arab quarter, to whom this ferocious warning was addressed. Meanwhile the city was being wrecked by naval bombardment and rocket launching planes.

Having seen the devastated city of Port Said for myself, I was appalled at the hypocrisy or sublime ignorance of the British politicians who claimed that the British and French commanders were hampered by their instructions to make sure that as few civilians as possible should be hurt, that the damage should be as small as possible, and that "air raids were restricted to Egyptian air fields."

Far from this being the truth, the whole Arab quarter of Port Said resembled one of the ruined cities of Germany in the immediate post-war era. I looked over a vast expanse of flattened, charred remains and even larger areas of partially destroyed streets and gutted houses where the inhabitants who had escaped with their lives were poking about among the ruins. The total number of civilian casualties was not yet known when I visited Port Said on December 22, but was estimated at close to 10,000. Women and children had been machine-gunned as they fled from their burning homes, as witness the photographs taken by the Swedish photographer, Per-Olow Anderson, who managed to slip into Port Said while the carnage was on and counted the bodies of seventy children slain by bullets. His pictures were published almost everywhere in the world, including England, but excepting the United States. I met and talked with him in Cairo. The British had cut off the water supply and there was no electricity, and he saw doctors operating by candlelight with only one bucket of water in which to wash their hands. Meanwhile, the British-Cyprus radio was telling the Egyptians that they would continue to be slaughtered unless and until they got rid of Nasser.

British correspondents on the spot flatly contradicted Butler's statement to the House of Commons that only a hundred Egyptians had been killed and only 540 wounded. Two weeks after the fighting ended, the London *Times* correspondent reported from Port Said that "everybody here is still utterly at a loss to account for the official statement in London . . . when anybody could walk through the hospitals to see the wounded or past the cemetery where the bodies lay too long." Even the *Daily Express* correspondent wrote:

> The official figure of 100 Egyptians killed is stupid. Unfortunately I saw many more. I believe a fair estimate is around 1,000 killed, military and civilian; 5,000 wounded; 25,000 homeless. It would have been better to tell the truth.

This same newspaperman also described the "horrible situation" at a hospital he visited: "Two thousand casualties with no water and no medical supplies."

The terrible vengeance taken by the British when their commandos were fired upon, *after* the cease fire but before the Arab quarter knew about it, was reported by Denis Pitts in the *Daily Herald*. He wrote:

> The Commandos left and the bloody slaughter began. British and French tanks went into the Arab quarter. If a sniper was sighted, a shell was fired at the window where he had been seen. . . . Many people were killed in this way. Many more were burned to death. The Egyptians had been told by the 'Voice of Britain' to stay indoors. 'You won't get hurt,' they were told. . . . The Army could well have given the Arab quarter time to know that a cease-fire had been called.

I spent a day in Port Said with Lydia Oswald of the Hearst press the day the British and French forces withdrew from Suez.

Many of its inhabitants speak English or French, or both, and my knowledge of German enabled me to talk also to some of the Swedish U.N.E.F. forces who were guarding the barbed wire barricades behind which the British forces were embarking.

Everywhere the people clustered round us to tell their experiences and many of them expressed their gratitude to America. The most frequent remark I heard was shocked surprise at British behavior. "The French, yes," one educated Arab said to me, "we expected nothing better from them—but that the British should have behaved the way they did, that we cannot understand."

It was not only Britain's sudden and brutal attack which had killed, injured or rendered homeless so large a part of the population of Port Said, that disillusioned her many former friends and admirers in Egypt. It was also the behavior of her army after it had taken possession of Port Said. A Canadian woman from New Brunswick, married to an Egyptian engineer, told me how her apartment was wrecked by the British before their withdrawal, for no ostensible purpose except revenge. Since two of her three children are American citizens, having been born in the United States where she and her husband lived for many years, the American Consulate had offered to evacuate them all. She preferred to stay near her husband who was employed by the Suez Canal Company. When the bombing began, she had moved from their apartment to that of friends with a cellar which served as a shelter for seventy people, including thirty-five children. She had from time to time ventured back into her apartment to collect things she required and, except for shattered windows, had found it still undamaged and her possessions intact. On her next visit a British officer in charge at first refused to let her in, but was persuaded to do so when she said she was Canadian born. She then discovered her apartment in ruins: pictures smashed, carpets slashed, furniture broken, and her clothes and other possessions either gone or thrown on the floor in a messy heap. The young British officer in the building was ashamed when she told him that she knew her apartment had been sacked only after the British took possession, but told her they had had no means of knowing the owner was not an Egyptian.

This Mrs. (Willa) Elwi's husband had been wounded when machine-gunned from the air as he was driving to Ismailia.

I visited two of the hospitals in Port Said and talked to Western-educated doctors who had performed heroic feats in attending to masses of wounded civilians in the terrible days of the bombing. Dr. Ramsis Magaldi, the Inspector of Public Health in the Canal Zone, told me they were happy that they had been able to prevent epidemics by the use of twelve tons of DDT, of which they luckily had abundant supplies on hand. British and French troops had prevented medical supplies coming in. Lack of these, however, had not been their main problem, but the large number of the wounded, and the lack of water and light and bread, which could not be baked for many days. The nurses had, however, made cakes for the patients. Some hospitals had been wholly, and others partially, destroyed by bombs, shells or gunfire from the British fleet; but the main government hospital which had been a receiving center before "the invasion" had not been damaged. It was here that I sat in the courtyard and talked to a group of doctors. Outside the gates a crowd was waiting for a free distribution of food and soap by the Red Crescent. Four thousand of the homeless were being sheltered in schools; many more thousands had no shelter. No foreign aid had been given except for a private American donation of milk, cheese and butter.

In the afternoon we walked around the shattered Arab quarter under the bright sun. A life-size effigy of Eden labelled a "war criminal" dangled in the air from a rope hung across one narrow street. On the walls of many ruined homes one could still read defiant slogans which the British had not been able to obliterate. Nasser's picture was, of course, everywhere. On one long wall a painted message in huge letters read: *Cochons français retournez aux feux d'Alger.* We drove in a one-horse shay whose loquacious English-speaking driver took pains to have us stop and see and photograph the worst destruction. No one begged from us, but ragged children and adults gathered around and pointed to where their homes had once been in the vast flattened area near the sea, our coachman translating what they said.

In the hour interview I had with Colonel Nasser on December 19th in his retreat near Cairo, he expressed his gratitude to America, and said:

> We knew we were too weak to resist the combined force of the Anglo-French and Israeli attack, but we had confidence in Western moral force to defeat British power politics. For the first time, we were able to put our case to the world and consequently, Western morality defeated aggression.

"We have been accused," he continued, "of being unmindful of world consequences. So far is this from being the truth that we knew we were running a grave danger when we trusted to the moral opinion of the world, exerted through the U.N., instead of taking the risk of unleashing a world war."

He also told me that when he had made his November 9th speech thanking America and Russia, the people had applauded Russia. "Our people," he explained, "are the most mistrustful in the world. They have been subject to too many invasions by the West: first Napoleon, then the British, and now again the French and the British together with Israel. Before 1948, America, unlike England and France, was held in high esteem, but since then, thanks to President Truman's all-out support of Israel, we became suspicious of the United States as well. But now, two months after the Anglo-French attack, we are beginning to be convinced that the policy of the U.S. has changed. We are now ready to believe that Israel is not acting for the United States."

In contrast to Nasser, it was the United States Ambassador to France, Mr. A. C. Douglas Dillon, who insisted that Russia, not the United Nations or the United States, had saved Egypt. In a radio interview on C.B.S. on December 11, 1956, Mr. Dillon said it was not moral suasion, but Soviet threats, which had caused Britain and France to call off their campaign against Egypt. Anxious to assure France that, right or wrong, she could count on America, the American Ambassador gave more aid and comfort to the Communists in the Middle East than any Arab, by telling the world that the USSR, not the United States, was Egypt's savior. Fortunately, the State Department soon thereafter removed Mr. Dillon from his post in Paris, but the damage he had done lived after him. Nor was he the only American to express the view that Egypt owed her salvation to the USSR. For instance, Mr. Eugene Rabinowitch, editor of the *Bulletin of the Atomic Scientists,* wrote in its January 1957 issue:

> A few days after the Anglo-American ultimatum to Egypt, Britain and France were presented with a virtual ultimatum threatening by clear implication, the air-atomic destruction of both countries if they failed to call off the Suez expedition.
>
> This demonstration of the power of air-atomic deterrence is a turning point in history, and we should not be distracted from recognizing its significance by incidental events, such as the diplomatic pressure of the United States . . . or the speeches given, and the resolutions passed in the United Nations.

> What England and France did *not* anticipate was a readiness of the Soviet leaders to unleash all-out atomic war in response to a local conflict so far from their own borders.

Drew Middleton of the *New York Times,* however, reported from London on January 31, 1957, that the most important of the many factors that caused England to agree to a cease-fire was the attitude of the United States, other factors being the attitude of Canada and British public opinion.

No doubt it was a combination of all these factors which caused Sir Anthony Eden and his Tory friends to give up his dream of re-establishing British imperial power in the Middle East by "teaching the Wogs a lesson." The damage he had done to British honor, interests and prestige, and to the anti-Communist cause everywhere in the world is incalculable. But his failure has taught a lesson which is likely to prevent any British Government from again diverging from the wise policy followed elsewhere in recent years: that of gracefully relinquishing imperial privileges and powers in Asia and Africa, and making friends of those who used to be her subjects.

IV

IN THE HOLY LAND

UNDOUBTEDLY PRESIDENT NASSER belongs to the species described by the French as "un animal très méchant, quand on l'attaque, il se défend."

But it is precisely because he defends himself when attacked that he has become a hero and a symbol to the Arab people who for so long were unable to defend themselves against aggression or to throw off the yoke of foreign conquerors.

As Nejla Izzeddin, the brilliant and eloquent Arab woman who wrote *The Arab World,* said to me in Beirut in December 1956:

> Nasser symbolizes in himself the desire of the Arabs to be strong and free, as we used to be in the days when Arab civilization was a light to the world, and our military prowess was unparalleled. Our hopes can be fulfilled only if the Arabs, who constitute nearly a hundred million people, are reunited, and our social, political and economic life reformed and modernized.

Dr. Izzeddin belongs to the Druse sect, or religion, whose members are the only non-Jewish citizens of Israel who enjoy equal rights with the Jews. Our host and hostess the evening I spent with her in Beirut are Roman Catholics. Three of the other guests at the apartment of Robert and Georgette Kfoury, whose hospitality I enjoyed in Lebanon, were Moslems, and one of them was a cousin of the Lebanese Prime Minister. None of them considered that either their religion, or the artificial divisions of the Arab world imposed on them by the West, as of any significance as compared to the fact that they were all Arabs. Much as they, and others I met in Lebanon and Jordan, might disagree about Nasser; whether or not they considered that Egypt had taken the wrong path by securing Soviet Russian arms and political support; and whether or not they considered that Nuri Es-Said of Iraq is pursuing a more sophisticated and intelligent policy more likely to succeed than Egypt and Syria's intemperate nationalism—they one and all agreed that the paramount fact in the Arab world today is the desire for strength through federation and reform.

All of them spoke French as fluently as Arabic. None of them were anti-American. But they all either failed to understand, or were mad at the injustice of the label "anti-Western" applied to all Arabs who oppose French colonial rule in Algeria and the Israeli threat to the Arabs.

As Dr. Izzeddin said:

> Our aspirations are in line with the world trend toward integration. The cause of Egypt after she was attacked was espoused by the U.S. and the U.N. because of the world's desire for justice and freedom. Why then do you accuse us of being anti-Western because we seek justice and equality for the Arab people?

Nor did anyone disagree with the view that Nasser enjoys immense prestige and popularity in every Arab country. Even the Arabs who deplored it recognized the fact admitted by such anti-Nasser columnists as Joseph Alsop, who reported from Beirut that the Egyptian President "is still for good or ill the biggest figure in the Arab World." The same columnist, after visiting Baghdad, also reported, in a column datelined May 22, 1957, that there is a lack of "true popular enthusiasm for the wise (oil financed) Iraqi development program," whereas Arab leaders such as Nasser "win mass support" by what Joe Alsop describes as "venemous but powerful emotional appeal to ancient and justified hatreds."

The key word is "justified," as Mr. Alsop himself admitted when he further stated that such pro-Western Arabs as the rulers of Lebanon "fear Nasser despite their own strength" because "these hatreds have a solid base in the countless tragedies of Middle Eastern history."

One needs to visit the Middle East, as well as study the historical record, in order to appreciate the tragic truth of these words, which are the more impressive because Joe Alsop is one of the many American columnists and commentators who harbor the most friendly sentiments toward Israel, France and England.

The wrongs of the Arabs are not only ancient, but a part of their present lives. "What we resent most," said Nejla Izzedin, who holds an American PhD. degree, and who speaks as beautifully as she writes, "is the double standard you apply to us and the Jews. The latter are always being presented as 'fighting for freedom,' but our Arab struggle is called 'fanatical nationalism.' "

A few days later I was driving from Jerusalem to Bethlehem in the evening, with another Lebanese, Dr. A. R. Labban, who runs a mental hospital for Arab refugees in this part of Jordan. We were stopped several times by uniformed Jordanian home guards, who work their farms or tend their flocks by day and guard them by night from Israeli attack. Two of them, after recognizing Dr. Labban and having been assured that I was neither Israeli nor British but American, asked us for a lift to the next check point. These and others we spoke to carried Russian tommy guns.

With Dr. Labban acting as my interpreter, I asked each of the dozen or more guards we met what they thought of Russia, Communism and Nasser. The answer was always more or less the same. "Russia? Communism?" they replied. "We don't know anything much about either; but we now have guns for the first time to defend our lands and families against the Israelis who used to attack us with impunity; so Russia must be our friend."

When I asked them how they felt about Nasser, or why they thought so much of him, their aquiline faces lighted up, and their dark eyes glowed as they replied, "He is straightforward and brave"; or "we believe in Nasser because he is straightforward."

In the moonlight on this ancient road which skirts the Mount of Olives to the left as one travels to Bethlehem and then twists its way along the side of the hills south of the Holy City, these answers by simple men guarding their families by night told the story more eloquently than any book.

The reason why straightforwardness or trustworthiness was regarded as the primary virtue of President Nasser of Egypt by these Arab farmers and shepherds was apparent to me on that unforgettable night on the road to Bethlehem, because of what I had just learned in a long talk with Mrs. Vester in Jerusalem. This wonderfully understanding, compassionate, and courageous old lady hails from Chicago, but she has spent more than forty years of her life in Palestine, where her father founded the American Colony in Jerusalem in 1881. Bertha Spafford Vester, whose husband died several years ago, has carried on their joint work and now presides over the Spafford Children's Hospital situated above the Gate of Damascus and helped by the Ford Foundation. The larger general hospital owned by the

American Colony was lost when the State of Israel, in defiance of the United Nations occupied the modern half of Jerusalem. Altogether, eight mission hospitals belonging to different Protestant and Catholic missions situated in Western Jerusalem are no longer available to the Arab population. Yet the latter are not allowed to make use of the Hadassah hospital in the demilitarised zone, which stands empty except for a guard.

"The Arabs," Mrs. Vester said to me, "consider that the breaking of one's pledged word is shameful. They used to respect the British as people who had the same sense of honor as themselves but have been bitterly disillusioned. When I first came to the Holy Land with my husband, an Arab who wished it to be believed that he was speaking the real truth and nothing but the truth would say 'English truth.' But today, when he says 'English truth' he means a lie."

Several years ago Mrs. Vester wrote a book called *Our Jerusalem* about her life with her husband in the Holy Land, published by Doubleday Doran. Her final chapter, which gives an account of how the Arabs have been deceived and cheated by the West, as also of the crimes committed by Israeli terrorists against the Arabs, was deleted by her publishers from her book. She gave me a copy of this chapter, which she had printed in pamphlet form at her own expense. From her lips, for the first time, I heard the terrible story of the Israeli massacre of the inhabitants of the village of Deir Yaseen which caused thousands of Arabs to flee and become refugees in Jordan and the Gaza Strip.

With tears in her eyes even after so long a time, Mrs. Vester told me how the Irgun forces had rounded up the whole population of this Arab village, machine-gunned the men and also many women and children, and how, afterwards, loud speakers mounted on jeeps or armored cars had paraded western Jerusalem warning the inhabitants that, if they did not get out at once, they would suffer the same fate as the people of Deir Yaseen.

"In my hospital," she said, "I took in fifty babies under two years old from the martyred village of Deir Yaseen."

As she told me, and as she wrote in the expurgated chapter of her book:

> While I was registering these babies and listening to the horrible recital by the women of what they had been through, a small boy about four years old stood by me. Seeing that I was not an Arab, he gave one shriek and said, "Is she one of them?" and fainted. I ran to get water to revive the child but when I returned with the water, I found that he was dead.

Mrs. Vester's graphic and heart-rending account of the horrors she witnessed in 1948, when fifteen thousand casualties passed through the casualty clearing station of the American Colony in Jerusalem, only incidentally mentioned the dangers and hardships which she and her family and co-wokers endured. The main house of the American Colony was demolished by a Jewish mortar bomb. They were in the direct line of fire between the Zionists and the Arab "ragtag and scalawags" who fought them. The British-commanded Arab Legion in Jordan delayed its advance so long that Zionist gangs were enabled to sack the Arab quarter of the city wherever they were not prevented by the desperate resistance of such of its inhabitants as could lay their hands on any kind of weapon. Some American missionaries were killed, or died of their wounds because no doctors were available to attend to them. But, Mrs. Vester said, the Arabs respected the Red Cross flag and, because the followers of Mahomet do not fire on women, she had been able to halt them from molestation of what remained of the American Colony's buildings after the Israeli shelling.

The Deir Yaseen massacre was only just one of a series. In the years that followed, murder and pillage were committed by both sides in the bitter struggle between Israel and the Arabs. For instance, in October 1953, Israeli armed forces swooped down on the border village of Kibya, massacred sixty-six Jordanians, injured many others, and blew up scores of buildings. The Arabs meanwhile committed similar horrible crimes, but with much greater adverse publicity in the American press.

It is frequently said that the Arabs have only themselves to blame for the loss of yet more territory than was awarded to Israel by the United Nations, because they attacked the new State and were defeated. This assertion ignores the historical record. As Dr. William Ernest Hocking, Professor Emeritus of Harvard University, has written, the Irgun, the Stern gang, and the Haganah—forerunner of the Israeli Army—had started their terrorist activities long before the British evacuated Palestine, and came out from underground to attack Arab villages and towns, masacrering their inhabitants or driving them out, immediately following the November 1947 United Nations resolution. In Professor Hocking's words:

> The documented facts leave no doubt that Israel was the aggressor. . . . Before the British Mandate ended on May 14, 1948, and two months before the State of Israel could legally be proclaimed . . . the Zionist-Israeli armies had already illegally occupied much of the territory reserved for the Arab State. . . . During this six month period of hostilities 300,000 Arabs were driven out of their homes by terrorist tactics and became refugees—contrary to every human decency. The impact of these sufferings extended in deep waves to the entire Arab world. Sympathy and an outraged sense of justice became a determined antipathy to Israel not to be cured by diplomatic placebos of essentially uninformed statesmen.

The world has supped so full on the horrors perpetrated by the Nazis and Communists that we have become insensitive, or we condone crimes against humanity committed by our friends or by those who were formerly persecuted. But if ever the fatal cycle of cruelty and crime and retaliation is to be broken, we must realize that atrocities remain atrocities even when committed by our allies, or by those whom we pity because they themselves have been persecuted and victimized. Otherwise mankind will revert to barbarism, in spite of all its wonderful achievements in science.

Mrs. Vester's compassion for the Arabs, whom she saw defending their homes with old blunderbusses and swords against Israeli forces equipped with Western weapons, had not caused her to become an "anti-Semite"—which is a meaningless term when applied to the conflict between Arab and Jew, who originally belonged to the same "race"; nor did she wish that the Arabs might have their revenge on the Jews. She realized that the Jews who committed the atrocities she witnessed had been brutalized, or driven into evil courses, by their own treatment by the Nazis, or by the persecution they had suffered elsewhere, and by their desperate situation in an Arab world rendered implacably hostile by the partition of Palestine. She told me that many Jews in Jerusalem were intimidated into supporting the terrorists among them who in their treatment of the Arabs were emulating the Nazis from whom they had escaped. One of her best nurses, a Jewish woman, had telephoned to her while the Jews and Arabs were fighting for possession of Jerusalem to say that she could no longer work in the American Colony hospital. Mrs. Vester assured her that she had nothing to fear from the Arabs, who trusted her completely after her thirty years of service to them in the hospital. But the Jewish nurse replied: "It is not the Arabs I fear but my own people."

In 1954 President Eisenhower received Mrs. Vester while she was visiting Washington and had a long talk with her. It is not inconceivable that her account of the tragic Israeli-Arab dispute helped the President in his decision two years later to defy Zionist, British and French pressures during the election campaign in November 1956.

Mrs. Vester's American-born son has become a naturalized British subject. Her daughter is married to a British Conservative M.P. In Jerusalem during our long talk she told me how worried she had been lest she become estranged from her family following Britain's aggression against Egypt. But to her great joy her son-in-law was one of the Conservative Members of Parliament who opposed Eden's policy.

I left Mrs. Vester after my three-hour talk with her in her home in Jerusalem, after arranging to visit her hospital at 6 A.M. the next morning. I had been invited to spend the night with Dr. Mahmoud Tahrer Dejani and his wife, also a doctor, at their house adjoining the Arab National Hospital in Bethlehem, which is also the only modern equipped hospital available to the adult population of the old city of Jerusalem.

The Dejanis, whom I had met, thanks to my publisher, Henry Regnery, and to Dave Collier of the American Friends of the Middle East in Chicago, had formerly been wealthy residents of the modern, west side section of Jerusalem. After being driven out by the Israelis in 1948 with the loss of all their possessions, they had started their refugee hospital in Bethlehem with financial support from generous American friends in Chicago. One of their sons works for the United Nations, which provides the Arab refugees with the minimum of food to sustain life—about 1700 calories—at a cost of 8 cents a day. Dr. Dejani's hospital endeavors to provide medical services for these destitute people but finds it difficult to cope with the multitude of sick and undernourished Arab refugees. I was enabled to appreciate both the generosity of individual Americans, the gratitude of the Arabs towards them, and the selfless dedication of the educated Arabs who devote themselves to the service of their countrymen, by the day and night I spent with the Dejanis and their relatives and friends in Bethlehem.

It was also in Bethlehem that, through a personal experience, I learned that President Eisenhower's stand on Suez had won goodwill for America among the Arab refugees living out their miserable, and almost hopeless, existence in caves and tents and mud huts within sight of their former homes in Israeli territory. As I entered one of the refugee camps on a hill on the outskirts of Bethlehem with Dr. Dejani's young son, a group of Arabs glowered at me with such unmistakeable hostility that I felt ashamed. But half an hour later, as we came back to the main road after my inspection of the camp, I was greeted with smiles by the same group of Arabs. This I found was because the Arab driver of Dr. Dejani's car, whom we had left behind, had assured them that I was not English, but American.

None of the refugees in this camp or elsewhere asked me for alms. In contrast to India, where you cannot park your car for a moment without being surrounded by beggars, these destitute Arabs retain their dignity and ask for nothing but justice.

As we sat wrapped in blankets before a small fire in his little stone house that night, Dr. Dejani said to me:

> We are with the West if you will treat us fairly—if not, come what may.
>
> Russia has not spent a dollar in the Middle East but is gaining influence nonetheless. America which is spending so much gets little thanks, because her dollar aid helps only to make the rich richer, or is dissipated in futile projects. Take for instance, your Point 4 Program. What has it done for the people of Jordan? It has provided funds to build a palace in Aman and for the construction of a government research laboratory, none of which visibly benefit the people. We need schools and colleges and small scale industries, which can enable us to help ourselves instead of being dependent on U.N. or U.S. charity. But your people seem to be more interested in providing us with luxuries, or the latest, most modern scientific research institutes. Here, I

> train practical nurses who will at least be capable of attending to the wants of the sick. But the U.S. and the U.N. send us Western-trained specialists and nurses whose high standards cannot be applied in a backward country, and who, because they cannot speak Arabic, cannot even communicate with our people.

In 1949-50, while directing the medical services of Jordan Dr. Dejani had been producing vaccines locally and had hoped to secure Point 4 aid for this purpose. Instead the United States had preferred to give $100,000 for building a research laboratory. Yet, obviously, as he said, in a country whose medical services are in their infancy the great need was not for research laboratories, but for hospitals, nurses and doctors whose standards are not too high to enable them to cope with the needs of a people on a low level of subsistence in need mainly of "district nurses" and general practitioners rather than specialists.

These may be minor matters as compared with the other mistakes or iniquities of American aid, but are nevertheless of interest and importance to Americans who wonder why all their generosity to foreign countries reaps so poor a reward. Dr. Dejani and his wife, sons and sons-in-law were far more emphatic on the subject of America's backing of Israel against the Arabs, than in their criticism of the manner in which Point 4 aid is given in the Middle East. Like the Kfouris in Beirut and other Arabs I met who know America, they are our friends and are striving to keep their countries on our side. But they were outraged by the double standard applied by the American press to Arab and Jew, and deplored our support of French colonialism in North Africa.

In the privately printed last chapter to her book, deleted from the American edition by her American publishers, Mrs. Vester emphasizes the fact that there was no trouble between Arab and Jew in Palestine prior to the creation of the State of Israel—regarded as a threat to all Arabs, thanks to her expropriation and expulsion of 700,000 of them from Palestine, her aim to bring in millions more Jews, and her organization as a military state.

> It is strange [Mrs. Vester writes] that the very people who suffered most from Hitler's racist theory concerning the German people, should use a similar theory to justify Zionism. Indeed just as there is no "pure German race," so there is no pure Jewish race. . . . The people who profess the Jewish faith are a mixture of many races. . . . The original Palestine Semitic strain is but one of many. . . . To speak therefore of the "return" of Jews of so many non-Palestinian strains to Palestine is absurd; they never came from Palestine in the first place. . . . It is indeed curious that liberals the world over who are loud in their condemnation of racist theories should have lent their support to as unreal a racism as any yet propounded.

No doubt, my reaction to my experiences in Jordan is "emotional." The same could be said of American reaction to the crimes and cruelties of Nazi Germany and Communist Russia. As I see it, hatred of oppression, compassion for the wronged and unfortunate, and the desire for justice are the attributes which raise us above the brutes. We sink back into barbarism, however, when we demand an eye for an eye, or let our emotions run away with us and lead us to revenge wrongs by their repetition. We must beware of letting sympathy with the Arabs cause us to do injustice to the Israelis. This would be to fall into the same error as President Truman when his sympathy for the Jews caused him to use American influence in the United Nations to recompense Hitler's victims at the expense of the Arabs.

As the British historian, Arnold Toynbee, writes in his *Study of History:*

> If the heinousness of sin is to be measured by the degree to which the sinner is sinning against the light that is vouchsafed to him, the Jews had even less excuse in 1948 A.D.

> for evicting Palestinian Arabs from their homes than Nebuchadnezzar and Titus and Hadrian and the Spanish and Portuguese inquisition had for uprooting, persecuting and exterminating Jews in Palestine and elsewhere at diverse times in the past. In A.D. 1948 the Jews knew, from personal experience, what they were doing: it was their supreme tragedy that the lesson learnt by them from the encounter with the Nazi German Gentiles should have been not to eschew, but to imitate some of the evils that the Nazis had committed against the Jews.

Fortunately there are still many Arabs who are prepared to forgive and forget the wrongs done to them if only America will now adhere to the principles which have made her great and free and strong. Dr. Dejani and his family, like many other Arabs who have studied in the United States and had experience of American generosity and desire to aid the poor or undernourished or oppressed peoples of all countries, are pro, not anti-American. But they find themselves classified as "anti-Western" because they are pro-Arab. Nor were the Dejanis personally revengeful against "the Jews," although they had been rich in Jerusalem before the Israeli Government confiscated all their possessions. Their main concern was to help the unending stream of sick and hungry Arab refugees who came to their hospital from the refugee camps or from Jerusalem, where the Arabs no longer benefited from the medical aid formerly provided by the Protestant and Catholic mission hospitals seized by Israel.

When I crept, shivering, into bed in the unheated Dejani house, and got up at 5 A.M., to wash in cold water prior to driving to Jerusalem, I was reminded of my austere youth in England following my family's ruin brought about by the 1914 War.

The Holy Land is a lovely land, unspoiled as yet on the Jordan side by the hand of modern man. In the pre-dawn light which erases the centuries, the barren limestone hills thinly spattered with green looked the same, I suppose, as in the days when Christ rode into Jerusalem on a donkey along the same route. Nearly two thousand years later there were no automobiles to be seen except ours. Only a few donkeys led by Arabs bringing vegetables to market. One felt oneself back in the morning of the world. In my semi-somnolent condition, I reflected that the problems and challenge of our modern world are in essence the same as those of earlier ages, when first the Prophets of the Old Testament, and subsequently Jesus Christ and Mohammed, called upon us to worship the same God and gave us the same basic principles of righteousness to obey, which have rarely been observed by either Jew, Christian or the followers of the Prophet.

After arriving at the walls of the Old City of Jerusalem and passing the narrow road which led to Calvary, the car left me at the Gate of Damascus. I entered Jerusalem on foot (since no vehicles can pass through its narrow gates and streets) and climbed up to the American Colony's Children's Hospital above the wall between the Damascus and Herod gates, along a narrow stone alley and many steps. The first rays of the risen sun were gilding the stone battlements as I surveyed the whole town from the roof of the hospital. Beyond the Gate of Damascus a new wall separates Arab from Jew, and behind it there is only grass and some shattered houses on the hill. The old city, where for many centuries the Arabs have guarded the Holy Places of Christians, Moslems and Jews alike, is now part of Jordan; beyond to the west I could see the outskirts of Israeli Jerusalem which is the modern part of the city.

My guide through the Old City was an Armenian Catholic nurse from Mrs. Vester's Children's Hospital. As we walked along the narrow streets, passable only by donkeys and people, on our way to the Church of the Holy Sepulchre, she told me how she and her family had lost their large and beautiful house in Western Jerusalem when they were driven out by the Zionists in 1948. Until then I had not known that Christians as well as Moslems had been expropriated and expelled by the State of Israel, which seized half of Jerusalem in contravention of the United Nations resolution that it was to become an international enclave. Thus in my ignorance, shared by so many Americans, I exclaimed, "Surely your family was not hurt, since you are Christians."

"But of course we were," she replied, "it made no difference whether one was Moslem or Christian; everyone who was not Jewish was driven out and dispossessed by the Israeli forces."

Already, in Lebanon, where half the population is Christian, I had learned that religion is not a major factor in the Arab feeling of resentment and hatred of the State of Israel.

In Beirut, the Kfouris, who are French-speaking Catholics, had told me that the worst thing Israel had done was to stir up long dormant religious antagonism and that they feared the Zionists might eventually succeed in setting Moslem against Christian, as they had already succeeded in dividing Arab and Jew.

No one can visit the Arab countries with an open mind without realizing that it is not religion or race, but resentment at injury and fear of the aggressive policy and Messianic pretensions of the State of Israel, which are the root cause of the seemingly irreconcilable conflict, misnamed that between "Arab and Jew."

The peoples of Iraq and Syria, Lebanon Jordan and Palestine, as also of Egypt and North Africa, are of many and diverse stocks or races which have intermingled and learned from one another ever since civilization began in the lands watered by the Nile, the Euphrates and the Tigris. Succeeding waves of conquerors or immigrants from the Arab desert to the South and the Persian highlands to the North further diluted the many racial and cultural strains of what we now call the "Middle East." Egyptian, Babylonian, and Persian conquests preceded those of the Greeks and Romans and all left a cultural legacy. Finally the Arab followers of the Prophet Mohammed in the seventh and eighth centuries placed an indelible imprint on these countries in spite of subsequent Mongol and Turkish conquests. The Arabs, unlike the Teutonic tribes who conquered the Roman Empire in the West, and the fanatic Christians who helped the barbarians to destroy Graeco-Roman culture, preserved the intellectual, philosophical and scientific heritage of the Mediterranean world for posterity. After conquering Rome's Eastern and North African provinces under the impulse and inspiration given them by the Islamic faith, they created a new civilization. In the words of George Antonius:

> It was a compound product resulting from a process of reciprocal assimilation; from the impulse which the Moslem conquerors gave to the resources of intelligence and talent which they found, disused and moribund, and quickened into life. In its external manifestations the new civilisation varied in each country, in keeping with the variations in the cultural aptitudes of the local populations. But two features were common to all: its faith and its language, with all that these implied of new standards and new outlook.

The Arabs, unlike the Teutonic kings converted to Christianity, did not kill those who refused to join the new faith. Instead, they made them pay taxes from which Moslems were exempt, a far more efficacious method of conversion. And while the new religion preached by the invaders was far from being universally accepted, the Arab conquerors gave an enduring unity to the peoples of what we now call the Near, or Middle East, by the gradual adoption of the Arab language as their mother tongue, either through intermarriage or Arab religious and cultural influences.

The process of racial "Arabization" had preceded the rise of Islam during the centuries before, when successive waves of immigrants or conquerors from the desert had intermingled with the many races of Palestine, Lebanon, Syria and Iraq. But it was only after the Arabs, inspired by their Prophet, established their Empire over the lands they had formerly only infiltrated or partially conquered that the many peoples of diverse racial origins, from Iraq to Morocco, were given an enduring entity—not so much on account of their adherence to the Moslem faith, which was by no means universal, but through their adoption of Arabic as their mother tongue.

Edward Atiyah, a Lebanese Christian Arab, in his illuminating book in the British "Pelican" series, ascribes the Arab cultural ascendancy in the Middle East and North Africa as "the joint creation of the Moslem religion and the Arabic language," which he describes as "one of the finest and most expressive forms of speech ever fashioned by the mind and tongue of man."

Who shall say, Edward Atiyah continues, how successful Mohammed would have been in preaching his new faith, "if the minds and ears of the Arabs had not become, through the love and practice of poetry, so susceptible to the magic" of the language he spoke and which is now that of a hundred million people in Asia and North Africa?

Beyond the spread of the Arabic language, which has given an enduring sense of unity to all the peoples from Iraq to Morocco, there is the yet wider sense of community of all those who have adopted the Islamic religion. Persia and Pakistan were never Arabized, but they reacted similarly to the dispossession of the Arabs in Palestine to make way for the State of Israel, and similarly against the Israel-Anglo-French attack on Egypt. And Iraq like Egypt has helped the Arab resistance to French rule.

Between the Christian West and the Moslems, whose religion

stems from the same roots as ours, no such barrier exists as between us and India, whose animistic primeval religions, superstitions, mysticism, and stratospheric philosophies of her wise men combine in a way that defies Western comprehension.

When I came to Pakistan and Iran, Lebanon, Jordan and Egypt, after a six weeks residence in India, I felt I had come home to a world I understood, because, in spite of the wide divergence in European and American history, social, and economic organization and political concepts, the Arab world is closely akin to us in the origins of its culture and religion. We are all in greater or lesser degree the inheritors of the legacy of civilization left to us by Babylonians and Egyptians, Persians, Greeks and Romans, Jews and Arabs.

As I learned in the Holy Land, and from the studies which my short stay in the Middle East impelled me to make, the Islamic religion constitutes less of a barrier between "East and West" than the Zionist revival of the forfeited claim of "the Jews" as the Chosen People of God.

Americans, like Europeans, know little or nothing of the Islamic religion, but have memories of the Crusades, represented in history and literature as a war for possession of the Holy Land between Mohammedan infidels and Christian believers in the God of Old and New Testaments. Few know that Mohammed's condemnation of the Christians was based, not on opposition to Christ's teachings, but on his view that the Christians had reverted to idolatry by regarding Christ as the Son of God, instead of as a prophet, and by their worship of the saints who had been permitted by the Catholic Church to take the place of the Graeco-Roman pantheon of gods. In chapter 2 of the Koran Mohammed says that the pagan idolatry of the many Greek and Roman gods should be wiped out, because "we follow the religion of Abraham the orthodox who was no idolator."

Unlike Judaism, Islam recognized Jesus as a Prophet. The

Koran regarded the Jews as collectively guilty because they had "slain Christ Jesus the son of Mary, the Apostle of God." But the followers of Mohammed did not persecute Jews—many of whom took refuge in Arab lands from Christian persecutors during the Middle Ages.

In the Koran the Jews are designated as the people who, descended like themselves from Abraham—to whose "seed" God promised the land "from the river of Egypt unto the great river, the River Euphrates"—betrayed their trust by reverting to idolatry during and after King Solomon's reign. They were therefore accursed by God for their infidelity and forfeited their claim, as their own Prophets had foretold. Since the phrase "to thy seed" included the Arabs descended from Ishmael, the Moslems consider they inherited the Promised Land after the descendents of Isaac had forfeited it.

I certainly am not qualified to record or judge the rights or wrongs of the Zionist claim to possess Palestine according to Scripture. Nor might their "spiritual" claim to dispossess the Arabs nearly two milleniums after the Jews were expelled by the Romans seem of any importance to American Christians, were it not for the support given the Zionists by fundamentalist Protestants who view the establishment of the State of Israel as a fulfillment of Biblical prophecy. Anyone interested in this subject should read Ilene Beatty's book *Arab and Jew in the Land of Canaan* (Chicago: Regnery, 1957), in which she has assembled the evidence in the Bible and history which contravenes the Jewish claim to have an inalienable right to possession of the Holy Land.

Miss Beatty's quotations from the Old Testament proving that the Jews, according to their own prophets, forfeited possession of the Promised Land "by ceasing to observe God's commandments" are usually ignored by a generation of Christians more ignorant of the Bible than their uneducated forbears in Europe.

Similarly with the historical record. The Zionist claim to take possession of Palestine as their homeland makes even less sense than if the Welsh or the Irish, because they are descended from the ancient Britons, should demand the right to rule over England. For the Canaanites, not the Jews, were the original inhabitants of Palestine.

Most of the Jews in Israel were taken into slavery in Babylon in the year 586 B.C. The remnant who survived were permitted to return to Palestine after the Persians conquered Babylon, and rejoined the Jews in Judah who had not been taken into captivity. But in A.D. 70 the Roman Emperor Titus decreed the destruction of Jerusalem and the dispersion of the Jews. And in A.D. 130 the remnants of the Jewish population of Judea were expelled by the Emperor Hadrian. Professor Alfred Guillaume of London University, as quoted by Stephen B. L. Penrose, President of the American University of Beirut, says: "Within the canonical literature of the Old Testament there is no prophecy of a second return after the return from the Babylonian exile." The last of the prophets died centuries before 70 A.D., the date of the destruction of Jerusalem by the Romans. From that time onward "the Jews" took refuge in neighboring countries, in Europe and North Africa, and, notwithstanding both their own and anti-Semitic propaganda, intermingled with other people and are now of as mixed or diverse racial origins as Americans. Their religion remained as the great force keeping alive their sense of unity. But today it is precisely the Jews who value and observe the principles of righteousness given them by God in the Old Testament who object to the Zionist claim to speak for all Jews. In the words of the President of the American University of Beirut:

> It is essential . . . that confusion be avoided between the secular, modern, political entity called Israel, and the Spiritual Kingdom which needs no earthly boundaries of time and space.

V

ISRAEL: OUR PROBLEM

THE SUEZ WAR, like a bombshell, awakened America to the explosive and threatening situation in the Middle East. Just as before 1950 Korea was only a remote place on the map, and the conquest of China by the Communists a matter of little concern until they attacked us in Korea, so also prior to the fall of 1956 most Americans knew little and couldn't have cared less about the Middle East. Suddenly we were awakened to the danger of being involved in yet another war far from home, and to the possibility of the outbreak of World War III in remote lands known mainly from the Bible or the movies.

Now that the spotlight in the Cold War has shifted to the Middle East, we can no longer afford to remain ignorant of the facts. Thanks to the Suez War and the Eisenhower Doctrine, keeping "the general area of the Middle East" free from Soviet domination has become yet another of our worldwide responsibilities.

Israel has become our problem. We cannot circumvent it by means of arms and economic aid given to those whom Sir Anthony Eden patronizingly called the "good Arabs." For regrettable or foolish as it may seem to us, it is a fact to be reckoned with that both "good" and "bad" Arabs fear Zionism more than Communism. Unless and until we convince them that America stands for a solution of the Arab–Israeli conflict in keeping with our principles of justice and equality—and that we also stand for an end to French colonial rule in Algeria—there can be no hope that the Middle East will concern itself with the basic struggle between Communism and the free world. We know that this struggle transcends all others; but, as an Arab proverb says, a drowning man is indifferent to the prospect of a thunderstorm. We cannot expect that so long as the Arabs see Israel as the clear and present danger which threatens them, and France as the visible oppressor of their "blood brothers" in Algeria, they can be induced to concern themselves with the far greater, but to them more remote, threat of being subjected to Communist tyranny. "Colonialism" as exemplified by France, but evoking also memories and fears of domination by Britain, constitutes the other great obstacle to the West's finding a basis of common interest with the Arab states and is dealt with in my next chapter.

America must give the Arab states a definite assurance that provided they will accept the existence of Israel within boundaries set by the United Nations and make peace with her, we shall not permit the Arab world to be drowned out by Anglo-French or Zionist imperialists; otherwise, the Arab world is likely to say "After me the deluge" as it is engulfed in the Communist ocean.

It is now imperative for our own security that we should formulate an American policy, made in Washington, instead of following, despite moments of brief opposition, policies made in New York, London, Paris, or Tel Aviv. This can be done only if we study the problem without prejudice or fear, and free ourselves from the illusion that all Jews are Zionists, who together with their Christian supporters have the power to decide elections in key states.

Up to now nearly everyone who so much as admitted that the Arabs have reason for their hatred and fear of Israel was in danger of being smeared as anti-Semitic, or even accused of Nazi sympathies. It has therefore been mainly Jews themselves who have had the courage to expose and denounce Israel's misdeeds, and to oppose Zionist influence in America; and these Jews, because they believe Judaism is a religion, not a political, racial or national movement, have been called "traitors" to their "race."

It is also a significant fact that the Jews who have had the courage actively to oppose Zionism are among those who never went along with the liberal friends of the Soviet Union. Notable among them is Rabbi Elmer Berger, Executive Vice-President of the American Council for Judaism, who wrote a most valuable, informative and courageous book, published in 1956, called *Who Knows Better Should Say So*. In an address he delivered at the Fifth Annual Conference of the American Friends of the Middle East in New York in March 1957, he said that it was incomprehensible to him that Western policy-makers could "hope to challenge Soviet influence without recognizing the centrality of the Arab-Israel dispute." He expressed the hope that:

> The realists—distinguished from the expedient-servers—will see that unless this sore in the Middle East is healed by a justice that is sensitive to the past and compensatory for the future, it will facilitate the Soviet Union's plan to infect the whole area with international Communism.

As Rabbi Berger also said, he was most troubled by the tendency of men "even at authoritative levels of our own government" to be either pro-Israel or pro-Arab, instead of their proclaiming "a clear, ringing, firm declaration of fundamental American policy for Arabs, Israelis and Americans to hear."

"If we continue to try and play God," he concluded, "choosing first the Arabs and then the Israelis, in frantic efforts to apply palliatives in order to avoid a policy of *American fundamentals* we shall not only *not* help the Middle East but we shall lose our own soul."

We must face the issue instead of running away from it. Although America has no desire to presume to play God, or to be the arbiter in the seemingly irreconcilable Arab-Israeli conflict, we must perforce attempt to find a solution which will do justice to both sides—or do as little injustice as possible to both. In the words of Alfred M. Lilienthal, another courageous American of the Jewish faith, "There will be no lasting peace in the Middle East until justice becomes more than a lofty-sounding word."

Dr. Fayez A. Sayegh, Acting Director of the Arab States Delegation Office in New York, who also spoke at the 1957 conference of the American Friends of the Middle East, is not only the most brilliant and forceful spokesman in America for the Arab world; he also knows us well, thanks to his having studied at the American University in Beirut for his B.A. and M.A. degrees, and subsequently at Georgetown University in Washington for his Doctorate in Philosophy. Dr. Sayegh is both pro-American and anti-Communist; but, in welcoming the Eisenhower Doctrine as "the beginning of a process of formulating an American policy for the Middle East," he warned that it could not be a substitute for assurances of security to the Arabs against "the danger of colonial aggression or Zionist expansion."

In Dr. Sayegh's words:

> The Eisenhower Doctrine leaves out of account the dangers which are, in the opinion of the Arabs, most imminent and most real. . . . The danger to our sovereignty and ter-

ritorial integrity comes from the predatory designs of European colonial powers and from the aggressive expansionism of Israel. In the past as well as in the present, it has been greedy colonialism and expansionist Zionism which have coveted our resources and intruded on our territories. . . .

Soviet aggression on the Arab world is viewed by most Arabs as remote geographically, unknown historically, and . . . unlikely to occur in the foreseeable future. . . . The silence of the [Eisenhower] Doctrine about colonial or Zionist aggression must be considered as likely to encourage such aggression.

As Dr. Sayegh and others have also pointed out, although Communism is alien to the Arab or Islamic mind, resentments against European "colonialism and Zionism" and disappointment at the failure of the United States to give more than lukewarm support to legitimate Arab national aspirations, could combine to render the Eisenhower Doctrine useless as a shield against Communist conquest.

This does not mean that America should abandon Israel. But it does mean that we should cease to be so prejudiced in favor of the surviving victims of Nazi persecution, or feel so guilty concerning Western anti-Semitism, that we refuse to do justice to the Arabs who, incidentally, are also Semites.

We considered it an invalid excuse that the Germans either said they had no knowledge of, or that they dared not oppose the Nazi liquidation of millions of Jews. Today, as Rabbi Elmer Berger points out, both Jews and Christians give material and political support to Israel, without having any conception of what Zionism is. I do not here mean to imply that Israel has perpetrated any such great crimes against humanity as Hitler. There is, nevertheless, a basic similarity in kind, although not in degree, between her treatment of the Arabs and the Nazi attitude toward the Jews. In both cases the conception of themselves as a "master race" or "chosen people" has led to the perpetration of injustices and crimes against "inferior" races. As Arnold Toynbee writes in Volume VIII of his *A Study of History*:

> The Jews' immediate reaction to their own experience was to become persecutors in their turn . . . at the first opportunity that had arisen for them to inflict on other human beings, who had done the Jews no injury, but happened to be weaker than they were, some of the wrongs and sufferings that had been inflicted on the Jews by their many successive Western Gentile persecutors during the intervening seventeen centuries. . . . The Arabs in Palestine . . . became in their turn the vicarious victims of the European Jews indignation over the "genocide" committed upon them by their Gentile fellow Westerners in A.D. 1933-45.

Because of the above-quoted text and other passages from his writings, Arnold Toynbee has been denounced as an anti-Semite, although he made it clear that "the impulse to become a party to the guilt of a stronger neighbour by inflicting on an innocent weaker neighbour the very same sufferings that the original victim had experienced at his stronger neighbour's hands" is not a Semitic or Jewish characteristic, but one unfortunately common to all mankind.

The fact that the Arabs have been made to pay compensation for Nazi crimes, and for centuries of persecution or discrimination against Jews in Europe, is all the more unjust because until the State of Israel was carved out of their territory, they had lived in amity with the Jews among them. In general they have shown far greater tolerance for those who professed other faiths than Christian Europe during most of its history. And even today, with the exception of Iraq, there have been no mass expulsions of Jews from Arab countries to match Israel's treatment of her Arab population.

As Alfred Lilienthal writes in *There Goes the Middle East*:

> In Egypt, Jews lived for millenia side by side with followers of Islam—some of them descendants of ancient Hebrews whom Moses left behind in his exodus. Others fled to Egypt following the first destruction of the Temple in Jerusalem at the hands of the Babylonians. In 250 B.C. Philo tells us there were more Jews in Alexandria than in Jerusalem. Jews gained sanctuary in Egypt from Christian persecutions in Spain and Portugal in the 15th Century, from Soviet excesses at the time of the Russian Revolution and from Hitler's racial persecution. The invasion of Egypt by Israel on October 29, 1956, no doubt brought to an end this Egyptian sanctuary for the Jews of the world.
>
> But what has taken place in Egypt in the wake of the Israeli-British-French aggression has not been anti-Semitism. There has been no discrimination against Jews as Jews, but an identification of Jews with Israelis whom the Arabs oppose on political, not religious grounds. Israel is regarded by Egyptians as a foreign colonial power whose leadership and funds come from Europe and the United States.

In view of these facts, Nasser has every right to get mad at the American press when charged with being anti-Semitic. In his own words, "How can I be anti-Semitic? The Egyptians are a Semitic people too."

At least they are probably as justified in claiming to be Semitic as the Jews, who are also a mixed "race" and no more all of "pure" Hebrew ancestry than Egyptians are all Arab.

Arab hostility against the State of Israel is not merely the result of the expropriation and expulsion of hundreds of thousands of Arabs from the territories awarded by the United Nations to the new State. The deep and abiding hatred and fear of the Zionists, in every Arab country from "pro-Western"

Iraq to "anti-Western" Syria and Egypt, is due as much or more to Israel's treatment of the Arabs who stayed, and her threat to impose her rule over others.

As the English author, Gerald Sparrow, writes in his book called *The Sphinx Awakes* (London: Robert Hale, 1957):

> I soon realised that the Egyptian attitude was based less on the plight of the Arab refugees than on the situation of what has become the Arab minority (formerly a big majority) in Israel. . . . In direct violation of the elementary principles of human rights, and of the specific provisions of the [U.N.] Partition resolution, the 175,000 odd Arabs who had stayed behind, after the expulsion of the great majority of their fellow countrymen, have been subjected to patent discrimination, in law as well as in practise.

In America, Israel is usually represented as a democratic Western-type state, and it is generally unknown that it has oppressive and discriminatory laws similar to those of the Nazis in Germany, only upside down. Indeed there never has been a State more openly and completely based on a racial myth.

Israel's 1952 nationality law automatically grants citizenship to all Jews, who have unrestricted right of entry by the Law of Return of 1952 and are also permitted dual citizenship—which enables some of them to remain Americans while also owing allegiance to Israel. The Arabs, on the other hand, can become citizens in the land of their birth only if they can prove continuous residence since the establishment of the Israel State, if they have some knowledge of Hebrew, and if they are approved by the Ministry of the Interior as worthy of Israeli citizenship. Moreover, even the minority who can qualify are distinguished officially as "Class B citizens."

They are not marked out by having to wear arm bands with a crescent, to match those with the Star of David emblem which Jews had to wear in Nazi Germany. But their identity cards, marked with the letter "B," enable the police to subject them to the many harsh regulations to which all Arabs are subjected, including a prohibition to travel even a few miles from home without a military permit.

The Arabs have for the most part been concentrated in areas under military rule—Galilee, the Negev and the "Little Triangle" where 145,000 of the total remaining 175,000 Arabs under Israel rule are compelled to live. The Israeli army in these areas has the authority to banish Arabs and confiscate their property, to remove whole villages from one zone to another, and to try all Arabs by court martial. Civil rights have virtually been suspended for the Arabs in Israel; and the harshness of the military rule under which they live is one of their main causes of complaint. Since they are unprotected by the right to trial by due process, individuals can be banished from their villages, or imprisoned by military court on suspicion of harboring infiltrators, or thrown into jail simply because they are regarded as trouble makers. In the words of Rabbi Morris Lazaron, as reported in the *New York Times,* "There is no *habeas corpus* for the Arabs in Israel." As this principled and brave Jewish Rabbi has also written:

> The military forces at times ignore even the decisions of the highest Israeli courts. For instance an Arab takes his claim to home or land to court. The court confirms his claim and orders his property restored. The military destroy the property on the grounds of "security" and no one does anything about it.

Thus it is not only the property of the six or seven hundred thousand Arabs who fled in 1948 which has been confiscated. That of many other Arabs still resident in Israel has also been seized. Whole Arab villages have been destroyed and their inhabitants forced to leave to make way for Jewish settlement.

Bedouin tribes have been deprived of the means of existence by being ordered to get out to make way for new Jewish settlements. Sometimes this is done as collective punishment for acts allegedly committed by some individuals. In other cases even this excuse is not given. Instead the military governor simply declares a certain area as a "prohibited zone" into which no Arab may enter and then applies the 1953 law which prescribes the confiscation of all Arab lands which the owners have failed to cultivate! To make it all very legal the Arab, first prohibited from cultivating his land and then deprived of it because he failed to cultivate it, is offered a token compensation amounting to less than a year's yield of his farm. The total areas so confiscated are estimated to amount to about a quarter of the total of 880,000 acres of Arab land expropriated by the Israeli Government.

Israel's justification for her treatment of her Arab minority is the state of semi-war, or armistice, between her and the Arab states. Most of the Arabs within her borders are, or must be presumed to be, in league with their relations and friends across the border in Jordan or the Gaza Strip who constantly raid her territory. Any State in Israel's situation would undoubtedly treat a minority belonging to a hostile nation as enemy aliens.

Israel's treatment of her Arabs, like her slaughter of other Arabs in border raids in retaliation for their retaliatory killing of her people, is all part of the tragic cycle which began in 1948. Opinions may differ as to who is most guilty of most massacres and crimes, but since Israel is stronger than her neighbors she seems usually to have come off best in the horrible count of how many lives each side has exacted from the other in revenge. The main difference is that whereas Arab murders of Israelis are well publicized in America, Israeli liquidations of Arabs are only occasionally reported in our press.

Non-Zionist American Jews and even some Zionists have been

shocked at what they found in Israel, and it has been mainly through them that some knowledge of the facts has seeped into American newspapers, which are generally too frightened of the consequences of being accused of "anti-Semitism" to publish the Arab side of the story. A recent example is the report in the *New York Times* datelined Tel Aviv, June 23, 1957, which says that Ben Gurion had that day "rejected advice by U.S. Jewish leaders to abolish favoritism for Jews in the acquisition of Israeli nationality."

A change in policy, continued the *Times* report, had been urged by a delegation representing the American Jewish Committee (which is not Zionist but has supported Israel and raised funds to finance immigration to Palestine). Mr. Irving M. Engel of New York City, head of the Committee, said, "his organization had crusaded for equal treatment of Jews throughout the world and consequently was embarrassed by the fact that when the Jews got their own State, their Nationality Act discriminated between Jews and non-Jews."

Mr. Engel was also reported to have remonstrated with Ben Gurion concerning statements by Israeli leaders which implied "that Jews abroad owed loyalty to Israel." This, he dared to say, "exposed American Jews to charges of dual allegiance."

In contrast to the Israeli treatment of her Arab minority, the 50,000 Jews in Egypt remained unmolested until the Suez War, with no discriminatory legislation of any kind to separate Jewish, Christian or Moslem citizens—a fact which, incidentally, also proves that most Jews in Arab countries are not Zionist. Even following the 1956 Israeli attack on Egypt, Nasser, whom the Zionists like to call an Arab Hitler, refrained from taking oppressive measures against Jewish Egyptian citizens. Had he interned all the Jewish population in Egypt, as America interned her Japanese citizens after Pearl Harbor, he could have claimed to be following, not Nazi but democratic precedent.

Instead, the Egyptian Government left Jewish Egyptian citizens free, and interned or expelled only enemy nationals and some others who had never become Egyptian citizens. Moreover, as I discovered in Egypt in December 1956, while alleged Israeli atrocities against the Arabs in Gaza were being played up in Jordan and Lebanon, in Egypt little was published about them by the government-controlled press in order to obviate any danger of mob violence against the Jews. Of course, the Egyptians, being human, have not refrained from taking revenge on some of the Jews among them, and many Jews now find it hard to make a living in Egypt. But there has been nothing comparable to the wholesale confiscation of German and Japanese private property by the United States, Britain and France during and after World War II. Nevertheless, it is Egypt which is accused of persecuting and driving out her Jewish inhabitants, whereas Israel is usually represented in the American press as a gallant little State bravely defending "its" territory, and even as having brought democracy and material advancement to her Arab "citizens."

Our double-standard judgment of Israel and Egypt is also seen with respect to their foreign policies. Nasser, who describes his policy as "positive neutrality"—whatever that means—is represented in the American press as "anti-Western" and as leading or attempting to forge a pro-Soviet bloc in the Middle East; and it has become customary for United States newspapers to couple "Egyptian and Communist" influences in Jordan and Syria as if they were one and the same thing. But Israel, whose policy has been just as positively, or negatively, neutral as Egypt's, is regarded as a reliable ally, and a bulwark against an advancing Communist tide. In actual fact she is not and never has been anything of the kind. On the contrary, Israel not only owes her very existence as much to Stalin as to Truman, who beat the Soviet dictator only by a short head in the race to recognize the new State in 1948. Israel is also the only State in the Middle

East with a legal Communist party and with a majority of pro-Soviet or "netural" members in her governing body, the Knesset, or Parliament.

In her July 1955 elections, 25 seats out of 120 were won by the Communist Party and their avowedly pro-Soviet allies in the Achidut Avoda and Mapam parties, whose foreign policy platform proclaims "friendship between Israel and the Soviet Union as well as other progressive forces of the world." In addition, 40 seats were won by the Mapai (Israel Labor Party), which defines itself as "a Zionist Socialist Party" aiming at the establishment of "a State planned economy," and whose foreign policy "stands for non-identification with any bloc." This neutralist socialist party, to which Prime Minister Ben-Gurion belongs, is by far the largest party in Israel. (The next largest, with 15 seats, is the near-fascist Heirut Party, founded by the Irgun terrorists and openly proclaiming its intention to dispossess the Arabs of more territory, its aim being "The territorial integrity of Israel within its historic boundaries on both sides of the Jordan.")

Thus out of a total of 120 members in the Israeli Parliament there is a majority of 65 who are either Communists and their fellow travelers or who proclaim their "neutrality" between the free world and the Soviet Empire. Prime Minister Ben-Gurion's Cabinet is a coalition which includes members of the fellow-traveling Mapam and Achidut Avoda parties, as well as his own party, the powerful left-wing socialist and neutralist Mapai. (Two members of the Mapam Party who resigned in 1952 gave as their reason, "There is practically no field in which Mapam acts independently without the overt or covert partnership of the Communists." Alfred M. Lilienthal, *There Goes the Middle East,* p. 20.)

The record also proves that the Israel Government is and has all along been as neutral against us as Nehru's India. This is demonstrated by the following facts:

Israel was one of the first nations to recognize Red China. She failed to send even a token force to fight in Korea; and, on November 21, 1951, Prime Minister Ben-Gurion sent a note to the Soviet Union assuring Stalin that Israel would never be a "member of any kind of union or agreement which pursues aggressive aims against the Soviet Union." Unlike Iraq and Saudi Arabia, Israel has refused to permit the Western Powers to establish an air base on her soil for the defense of the free world against Soviet imperialism.

In a word, Israel is just as suspect as Egypt insofar as its attitude to Soviet Russia is concerned. Whereas any action by the United States falling short of complete support of Zionist objectives arouses vehement denunciation in Israel and in powerful sections of the American press, whatever Moscow does or fails to do, Israel continues her endeavor to maintain friendly relations with the Soviet Power. This is not only because of Communist, left-wing socialist and neutralist influences in Israel. Nor is it mainly because of grateful remembrance of "Russia's support at the time of the establishment of the Jewish State, and the fact that the Soviet Government gave *de jure* recognition to Israel immediately after the proclamation of its independence," to quote the statement made by the Israeli Minister to Moscow in December 1953. Israel does indeed remember the support Russia gave her, including the delivery of arms in 1948 which helped her win the war against the Arabs. But the compelling reason why all parties in Israel continue to try to maintain good relations with the Soviet Government is the Zionist aim to "ingather" the two or three million Jews in the Soviet Empire. Thus neither the bomb which exploded in the Soviet Legation in Tel Aviv in February 1953, nor the Russian anti-Semitic campaign that year, nor even Moscow's espousal of the Arab cause in the United Nations in 1956 caused either a lasting rupture in diplomatic and other relations between Israel and the Soviet Empire, or any fundamental change in the attitude of Israel's powerful left-wing neutralist political parties.

In taking the initiative in resuming diplomatic relations, broken off by Moscow following the bomb incident, Israel asked only that the Kremlin permit Jews in the Soviet Empire to emigrate to Israel. Israel's ambition to "ingather" the Jews from everywhere in the world has placed the Soviet Union in the enviable position of being able to strengthen its influence among both the Arabs and the Israelis. The Arabs fear that Israel will be rendered stronger and even more intent on expansion by the influx of a million or more Jewish refugees from Russia, Poland and Roumania. The Arabs therefore hope to prevent this accession of strength to their enemies by establishing or maintaining and strengthening friendly relations with Moscow. And on the other hand, the Israelis can be counted upon by Soviet Russia not to join any Western alliance against her, because this would destroy their hope that Moscow will permit the emigration of her Jewish subjects to Palestine. Since such permission can only exacerbate the conflict between Israel and the Arabs to the advantage of Moscow, it is probable that a flood of Jewish refugees from the Soviet Empire will soon arrive in Israel. In any case, the net result is that Communist Russia is the only power which was ever enabled to utilize anti-Semitism to its political advantage among both Jews and their enemies.

According to Walter Z. Laqueur's article in the June 1957 issue of *Commentary,* while the Soviet Union has grown more and more hostile, Israel has "steadily refrained from effective political counter-action" and has continued "trying to persuade" Moscow of her "friendly intentions." Since *Commentary* is a publication sponsored by the American Jewish Committee, and therefore cannot be accused of being anti-Semitic or prejudiced against Israel, Mr. Laqueur's article is of particular interest.

Reporting on his recent visit to Israel, he says that "many of the old illusions about the Soviet Union are still current in Israel—most widely, of course, on the left, where the lessons of both Khrushchev's revelations about Stalin and of the Hungarian revolution have been learned only in part and with great reluctance." He notes that many members of the "traditionally fellow-traveling" Mapam (Socialist) Party reveal their disillusionment in private conversations, but "when it comes to public declarations" the Mapam Party "has been less outspoken in its condemnation of Soviet actions than Pietro Nenni in Italy or Jean-Paul Sartre in France," because it apparently "fears that it would have to repudiate Socialism if its confidence in the Soviet Union were shattered." Thus, Mr. Laqueur says, the Mapam Party "officially continues to support Soviet policies and goes on cooperating with the Communists and with their front organizations such as Partisans of Peace, the WFTU, World Youth Movement, etc., and tends to regard Russia's present hostility as a temporary aberration."

Whereas in Egypt and elsewhere in the Arab world there is fear that unless the Arab nationalists commit themselves irrevocably to Moscow, the Kremlin and the "Western imperialists" will gang up against them, in Israel this possibility gives ground for hope. As Mr. Laqueur writes:

> There are people around who point out that another sudden change in Soviet foreign policy—in this case, from hostility to friendship for Israel—should not be precluded. Many members of Mapam are firmly convinced that such a change of heart will come about when the Kremlin realizes that its policy in the Middle East represents a deviation from the sacred principles of proletarian internationalism.

Mr. Laqueur also reports that other Israeli groups expect that the Russians may in the end drop Nasser as a bad bet, not only because his military strength is less than Israel's but because his "attachment to the Soviet bloc is doubtful." As well they might, since Communist and fellow-traveler influence in Israel is evidently so much stronger there than in Egypt.

Some of the reasons why the Israelis are so ill-informed about Russia and Communism are given in this same article by Walter Laqueur. Israeli publications, he says, "compare rather unfavorably in make up and content with their Egyptian counterparts," and "Radio Israel . . . trails behind broadcasting in Egypt and other Arab countries." Consequently, he writes:

> Many Israelis turn to foreign books, magazines and newspapers . . . [and] all too often read the wrong publications . . . [because] the familiar publication is often the one expressing the traditional left position, which has been the position of many Israelis. . . . This is a matter of greater political importance than appears on the surface. The impact of periodicals from London, Paris, and New York is far greater in Delhi, Beirut or Jerusalem than in their own countries. . . . The influence on Israeli thinking of the London *New Statesman* or of a political journalist like Isaac Deutscher—each of whom has a decidedly slanted view toward world affairs and the nature of the Soviet regime—can hardly be overrated, and this influence extends to the highest levels of the Foreign Ministry. Such sources may be one-sided, they may have been proved wrong many times, but since nothing better is known, dependence on them remains strong.

I have quoted at such length from Walter Laqueur's article because the testimony of a Jewish writer in a Jewish publication concerning the strength of Communist or fellow traveler influence in Israel is far more convincing than any statement by the Arabs or other enemies of Israel.

Israel has now, it is true, endorsed the Eisenhower Doctrine, but with reservations and only after a long and stormy debate in the Knesset, in which Premier Ben-Gurion had to exert all his influence to prevent an adverse vote. The motion was finally carried by a vote of 59 to 5, with 39 abstentions, it having been agreed beforehand that the Mapam and Achidut Avoda parties might remain within the coalition government if they abstained from casting negative votes. They had strongly objected that acceptance of the Eisenhower Doctrine would involve Israel in the Cold War between East and West and that it might jeopardize the chances of the Jews in the Soviet Union being permitted to emigrate to Israel.

In his speech to the Knesset the Israeli Premier made much of the point that the Doctrine guarantees economic and military assistance to any nation in the Middle East attacked not only by the Soviet Union, but also by another nation *controlled by international Communism.* Since this might at some future date be chosen to mean Egypt or Syria, Mr. Ben-Gurion was able to use the powerful argument that it "strengthens the security of Israel."

The Premier also made important reservations which seem to render Israel's adherence to the Pact only formal or nominal. According to the *New York Times* report from Jerusalem, datelined June 3:

> Despite Israel's acceptance of the doctrine, her policy will be to continue to seek friendly relations with every "peace loving" nation without inquiring into its system of government, Premier Ben-Gurion said.
>
> *But in one vital respect Israel is different from other nations, he added. This, he said, is in her determination to provide a national home for the Jewish people.*
>
> Because of this, Israel's statement supporting the doctrine was different from most of the declarations made by other Middle Eastern nations, Ben-Gurion said.
>
> This difference was said to center on two points: Israel stated that she was opposed to any aggression from any quarter and that she entertained no aggressive intent against any nation; *she also refused to denounce any other nation.* [Italics added.]

The *Times* correspondent also reported that during the debate "the Eisenhower Doctrine was also attacked by the Herut Party, the extreme Right wing group founded by former members of terrorist organizations."

If it were only resentment at past and present injuries which prevents a reconciliation between the Arab States and Israel, it might be possible to bring peace to the Middle East by resettling the Arab refugees and raising the standard of living of the miserably poor people of the Arab East by means of generous American economic aid. Unfortunately no such comparatively simple solution of the problem posed by the State of Israel is possible, unless and until the Zionists abandon their aim to "ingather" millions more Jews from all over the world.

As Senator Ralph E. Flanders, whom it would be impossible to accuse of being anti-Semitic or illiberal, said in a speech he gave on May 9, 1957:

> One thing of which the Arab world needs to be assured is that limits will be set on immigration into Israel. Present policies of unlimited immigration—practically speaking of invited immigration which may be beyond the natural resources of the region—must be abandoned. There can be no peaceful relations in the Mid-East so long as Israel is prepared to flood its area with a population which will inevitably exceed existing living room. A peaceful Mid-East requires that by word or action this policy is seen to be abandoned.

Of course, as the Vermont Senator warned, if any adjacent countries make continued existence for their long established Jewish communities impossible, there would be justification for expansion of Israeli territory to make room for them.

Israel's "open-ended policy of immigration," in Senator Flanders' words, is the visible evidence of the basic problem posed for the Arabs:

> [The Arabs] would like to know whether or not they can deal with the nation Israel. Are they dealing with a

> nation like other nations of the Mid-East, or are they dealing with some broad-spread movement such as goes under the name of "Zionism" with its material support, and likewise its ideals and purposes, spread throughout world Judaism? For a peaceful settlement in the Mid-East the Arab nations must be convinced that they are dealing with a nation like themselves and not with some massive supernational organization.

Commander E. H. Hutchison, USNR, who was a member of the United Nations Truce Supervising Organization in Palestine before becoming head of the Israel-Jordan Mixed Armistice Commission in 1954, expresses the same view. "The Arabs," he writes in *Violent Truce* (New York: Devin Adair, 1956), "cannot but fear that the constant drive by leaders of Israel and world Zionism, for the ingathering of Jews, must mean eventual aggression by Israel for the acquisition of more territory."

The record justifies these Arab fears.

At the time of the Balfour Declaration, November 2, 1917, there were only 57,000 Jews in Palestine—most of whom accounted themselves Arabs while professing the Judaic faith. By 1922 there were still only 84,000 Jews, and they owned only two and a half per cent of the land. According to the November 1947 United Nations Resolution partitioning Palestine, the population of the Zionist State it established was to consist of slightly more Jews than Arabs—497,000 as against 485,000—but with equal rights for both. Today there are only 175,000 Arabs left in Israeli territory, while the Jewish population has increased to a million and three-quarters and now owns almost all the land. Moreover, the area taken by Israel by force of arms already exceeds by 36 per cent that assigned to the "Jewish State" by the United Nations partition plan. According to Arab calculations, about half of the dispossessed and destitute Arab refugees come from the areas Israel has occupied in defiance of the United Nations. Nor were all these extra lands taken as spoils of war in 1948. Many were seized by Zionist terrorist bands during the last months of the British mandate. Others were taken over during and since the cease-fire ordered by the United Nations. Today Israel has already taken possession of 20 million of Palestine's 26 million *dunums* of land. The means by which this has been accomplished were described by Dr. Stephen B. L. Penrose, President of the American University of Beirut, in No. 4 of the "Minaret" series of pamphlets, published by American Friends of the Middle East:

> On both sides dreadful deeds were committed but, in the main, the Zionists made better use of the terrorist tactics which they learned only too well at the hands of Nazi taskmasters. There is no question but that frightful massacres such as that which took place at Deir Yassin in April, 1948, were perpetrated for the major purpose of frightening the Arab population and causing them to take flight. The Zionist radio repeated incessantly for the benefit of Arab listeners "Remember Deir Yassin." It is small wonder that many Arab families began a hasty exodus from the battle area and from sectors which might soon become battlegrounds. Terror is contagious, and it built up the tremendous migration which has led to the results which may be witnessed in the refugee camps.
>
> When the military front was finally stabilized on lines which do not correspond at all to the original partition boundaries, there were nearly a million Arab refugees displaced from their homes or else rendered destitute by the descent upon them of hordes of Arab families fleeing from their native localities. Most of them fled so precipitately that they took with them only what belongings they could carry and generally only such funds as would last them for a period of a week or two.

One reason why this ousting of the original population by the State of Israel has either been condoned or excused in the United States, is the fact that, thanks to the movies, the word "Arab" conjures up the image of sheiks on Arab steeds, impersonated by Rudolph Valentino and his successors on the no-longer-silent screen, or pictures of Bedouin tribes riding camels, tending their flocks and herds and living in tents which they could easily fold when required to move elsewhere. Alternatively, the Arabs, thanks largely to Zionist propaganda, are thought of as semi-savage nomads, resembling Red Indians, raiding the pioneer settlements of peaceful farmers in Israel or French settlers in Algeria.

These images, although they are to a limited extent true as regards French, or formerly French, North Africa, are little more representative of Palestine today than Hollywood cowboys and Red Indians represent twentieth-century America.

A large part of the world which calls itself Arab was civilized, and included great centers of learning in the days when our forebears in Europe were barbarians. It was the Arab conquerors of the eastern provinces of the Roman Empire who preserved and eventually passed on to Europe the knowledge of Greek science and mathematics of which they made themselves masters, and which, thanks largely to the Arabic numeral system, modern man has developed to become master of the universe while remaining a slave to his passions. Yet today, few Americans even know that the majority of the people calling themselves Arabs, who have been dispossessed by Israel, were either urban dwellers or farmers whose skill and industry in raising crops or fruits from infertile or mountainous lands without benefit of modern science and machinery has been equalled in Europe only by the Italians and the part-Arab population of southern Spain.

True, under Turkish misrule Palestine, like Syria of which it was an integral part, fell into decay, and its cultivators were reduced to a condition of acute poverty and semi-servitude under a privileged landowning class supported by the Turkish Government. It is also true that the small area left to the Arabs by the United Nations partition of Palestine (now part of the Hashimite Kingdom of Jordan) consists mainly of desert; but in lovely Lebanon, which is like a huge garden, one can see the result of Arab skill and industry.

To return to the main point: While it is important for us to know what kind of people the Israelis have dispossessed and what kind of means have been used to dispossess them, it is more illuminating for us to know the proclaimed aim of Zionism. The Zionist vision is the creation of a State in the entire area which they call "Eretz Israel"—meaning thereby the whole territory of Palestine and Jordan, comprising territories eight times as large as those assigned to the Jewish State by the United Nations.

It is not only the Israel extremist nationalists in her second largest party, the Herut, who aim at her expansion up to and beyond her so-called "historic boundaries." Premier Ben-Gurion himself, writing in the Israeli *Government Yearbook,* asserts that the State of Israel has been "resurrected" only in "a portion of the land of Israel" and goes on to say:

> Even those who are dubious as to the restoration of the historical frontiers, *as fixed and crystallized and given from the beginning of time,* will hardly deny the anomaly of the boundaries of the new State. [Italics added.]

The State of Israel, according to its formal declaration when it constituted itself, is dedicated to the "Ingathering of the Exiles" —meaning all Jews from everywhere in the world dispersed nearly two thousand years ago by Rome.

In the words of Max Ascoli, editor of the *Reporter,* in his "Report on Israel," published in the July 11 issue:

> The tendency [of Israeli leadership today] is to date back the origin of Zionism—and therefore of Israel—to the series of events, approximately two thousand years ago,

> that forced the Jews to move away from the land then called Judaea. The Israeli leaders want to redress the wrongs the Jewish people suffered at the hands of Greek kinglets and Roman emporers.
>
> These leaders are a formidable lot. With trenchant relentlessness, secretiveness, and unending inventiveness, they have gotten around all obstacles, and have made their interpretation of destiny into the destiny that rules the lives of nearly two million human beings—as of now.
>
> Zionism, this man-made destiny for people called Jews, has succeeded in making Israel—a nation dedicated to what they call the Ingathering of the Exiles.

Actually, Mr. Ascoli could have said that the Israeli leaders tend to date back the origins of Zionism not two, but three thousand years, since it was only during the reign of King Solomon that the Jews ruled over the area today designated as "Eretz Israel." In pursuance of this fantastic aim she needs more land to accommodate the millions of Jews she is endeavoring to "ingather," and they in turn are expected to give her the military manpower to conquer the land she needs. Of course, she will never succeed in inducing all Jews to return to Judaea, since millions of them have been assimilated in the countries of their birth, residence or ancestry, have no desire to become subjects of the "Jewish State," and repudiate its Messianic pretensions. Only a handful of America's five million Jews, or of England, France and Italy's substantial Jewish population, have emigrated to Israel. But there are millions of other Jews, in North Africa and the Middle East where they are as desperately poor as their Arab neighbors, and in Eastern Europe where they are both poor and oppressed, who grasp at the chance of a free passage to Israel and the opportunity to acquire land or decently paid jobs. Hence the yearly influx, which rose to 239,076 in 1949 and, after a subsequent decline, is now proceeding at the rate of about 100,000 a year and expected to go higher.

Every immigrant of military age is at once trained as a soldier, and all immigrants are expected to dedicate themselves to the achievement of Zionist aims.

Can we wonder why the Arabs are afraid and want to destroy the State whose policy requires the conquest and expropriation of millions more of the Arab people? As Dr. Penrose writes:

> [In the light of their experience the Arabs] have no faith whatsoever in the desire of Israel for a peaceful settlement on any terms but her own, and they fear that such negotiations, if initiated, would only be used as a sounding board by Israel for further intensive propaganda in the United States and elsewhere. The public protestations on the part of Israel of a desire and a need for peace ring as falsely in Arab ears as do those of Russia to the western world. The parallel is almost exact.

The Arabs are further infuriated and given grounds for fear by what several eminent non-Zionist Jews have called the "Messianic pretensions" of Israel—her claim to represent a superior and older culture than any other nation—her "chosen people" complex.

The claims made by Israeli spokesmen to be a very special people are illustrated by an address given by Dr. Ebba Eban at Georgetown University on April 9, 1957. The Israeli Ambassador to the United States, ignoring Egypt, Babylon and China, not only claimed for the Jews "mankind's oldest tongue and culture" which "more than Greece and Rome have determined the spiritual evolution of all generations," but also said: "This planet passed from barbarism to civilization at the moment when it was touched in Israel by the lucid radiance of the Hebrew mind."

Continuing, he claimed that for three thousand years the Jewish people in their march across the stage of history "had been the standard bearers of order and progress in the universal design," and that Modern Israel "is something of intrinsic merit and interest in itself as a human phenomenon, as the unfolding of a great mysterious and inscrutable design of history."

It would be easy to quote other less restrained and scholarly statements by Zionists than the above speech by Ambassador Eban. But it is not my purpose here to do more than call attention to Israel's exaggerated pretensions, which recall Nazi claims to "Aryan" superiority and which her neighbors regard as constituting a menace to them similar to Hitler's to the Jews.

If Israel were merely a little State of less than two million people, the threat would be meaningless. It is on account of Zionism as "a massive supernational organization," seemingly backed by Jews everywhere in the world, that the menace it constitutes to its neighbors becomes something more than a mere figment of Arab imagination.

The Reverend Edward L. R. Elson, Minister of the National Presbyterian Church in Washington, D. C., and Chairman of the National Council of the American Friends of the Middle East, writes:

> [The Arabs] regard Israel as a protectorate of the United States and the new State as a projection of Western imperialism into the Middle East. . . . They were presented with a proposition along these lines: "We are going to give half of your land to strangers, but if you are decent about it and do not make trouble for your new neighbors, we may let you keep the other half of your land." It is against this background that disputes about water rights and fields on the borderline assume deadly importance. The Arabs, seeing the expanding population of Israel and knowing the flow of financial and moral aid from the West, live in fear of further expansion of Israel. Hence, their military budgets go beyond what the economy of small states can afford. Their political leadership turns to those who prom-

ise resistance. Their foreign policy has to be oriented away from those states which are considered responsible for the creation of the new state. And no Arab and very few Jews will ever doubt that America played a decisive role in the creation of the State of Israel.

Rabbi Elmer Berger, Executive Vice-President of the American Council for Judaism, in answering the question "Why the Arabs should be so unyieldingly determined that Israel should not occupy territory beyond the lines established in the 1947 Partition plan," said:

> Only those can understand who know what psychological patterns have been built into the Arab mind by watching the Zionist experiment grow from the vague Balfour Declaration, in which Arab rights were guaranteed, to a full-bodied nation with a powerful military establishment and rejecting the right of repatriation for Arab refugees. Only those who know and understand—in any degree equal to their understanding and knowledge of the psychological factors of Zionism—will comprehend why psychologically the Arab insists on remembering the history of this problem. . . . It is not enough to say the Arab remembers these —and his political agitators use them—to nourish vengeance and bitterness. This memory is the psychological reason why the Arab cannot start from any point in present history and just go on from there, to a settlement predicated upon some latest crisis, rather than an understanding of the history in which Zionism eroded Arab rights with a diplomacy of *faits accomplis.*

In an enlightening and moving passage from the same speech Dr. Berger drew attention to the fact that whereas Hitler had dramatized for the West the tragedy of insecurity and disability for the Jews, nothing as yet has dramatized in a comparable fashion for the West the tragedy of a colonial and imperial attitude "toward the people who endured these manifestations of Western development" so often "glorified by the West." In sum, the Arabs too have been oppressed and cannot forget it any more than the Jews.

Dr. Penrose expresses a similar view:

> The Arab peoples have deeply ingrained in their souls a feeling of the injustice which has been dealt to them ever since the First World War and particularly since November 29, 1947 [the date of the United Nations Resolution to partition Palestine]. "On top of that and associated with it is the deeper bitterness toward the United States and the United Nations out of whose action has developed the picture of destitution, demoralization and suffering which is constantly before their eyes in the refugee camps. Even if they would forget the past they cannot do so with this constant reminder. . . . They feel that this is a situation brought upon them from without and that it is therefore from outside the Arab world that justice and recompense must come.

It would seem only too obvious that we are in danger of alienating not only the Arabs but also the far larger Islamic world, because our most-favored-nation treatment of Israel does give grounds for the accusation that she is "the spearhead of Western imperialism which still endeavors to divide and rule." The Arabs see that Israel is subsidized by huge, tax-free donations by American-Jewish citizens and by United States grants far larger than our economic aid to the Arab States, which, in spite of Israel's small population, have made her militarily the most powerful State in the Middle East. This leads the Arabs to the false suppositions that America controls Israel, and that we are thus responsible for what she does. As I found during my brief visit to the Middle East, it was difficult to convince the Arabs that, although we pay the piper, we do not call the tune. Americans for sentimental reasons may like to hear music that evokes memories of King Solomon's temple;

but the tune that Israel plays with our permission, if not at our bidding, so grates on the nerves of Israel's neighbors that they are tempted to call in a Soviet "policeman" to throw both the piper and the sentimental visitor out.

Even if the Eisenhower Doctrine succeeds better than the Baghdad Pact in creating a strong "northern tier" of Islamic States stretching from Turkey, through Arab Iraq to Persia and Pakistan, this will avail us little if the Soviet Power is enabled to threaten the rear by forming an alliance with the "anti-Western" Arab States, and by continuing to play upon the grievances of the Arabs, succeeds in subverting the people whose governments are allied to us. In a word, the success of the Eisenhower Doctrine will depend upon the support of the Arab people.

In combatting Soviet influence in the Arab world we enjoy the great advantage that it does not derive from the out-dated Socialist sympathies with Soviet Russia which influence India, Japan and Israel. Since it does not derive from any ideological affinity but is mainly the result of Western actions and policies, the Communist danger in the Middle East could be dispelled if we would recognize and endeavor to remove its causes—Zionist ambitions and French colonialism.

I have not here mentioned British imperialism because there is reason to believe that following Eden's disastrous Suez adventure, Britain has reverted to the wise policy she has generally followed since World War II—that of ensuring the friendship of her former colonial subjects by gracefully relinquishing imperial rule. Thus there is reason to expect that England would join us in the endeavor to formulate an enlightened Middle East policy which would win the reformist forces of Arab nationalism to our side and thus confound the Communists. There are even indications that, as concerns Egypt, England may steal a march on us by resuming friendly relations, unfreezing Egyptian funds, and entering into close commercial relations, while America continues to treat Nasser as almost untouchable.

If England and America would get together again, unhampered by Tory dreams of re-establishing the "power and the glory" of the British Empire, or by Zionist influences in America, or by the pull of loyalty to France in her futile endeavor to suppress the Algerian Liberation Movement, we might together be successful in formulating and implementing a policy beneficial both to the Arabs and Jews, and even to France, who is being drained dry by the cost of the war in Algeria.

Such a joint Anglo-American policy could be successful without abandoning, or doing injustice to, the State of Israel.

Although few of the Arab government leaders dare say so publicly, in view of the inflamed state of public opinion, all of them know that, sooner or later, they will have to accept the fact of Israel's existence and come to terms with her. But they will never be able to do so unless and until Israel abandons her aim to "ingather" the Jews from everywhere in the world—the goal that enhances both her need for living space and her military capacity to acquire it.

During my interview with President Nasser, on December 19, 1956, in his retreat near Cairo, I was convinced that he is not an extremist who dreams of "driving Israel into the sea." He said that he had never called for the destruction of Israel and was anxious only "not to see Egyptians dispossessed of their lands and property and become refugees like the Arabs of Palestine which was the prospect they had faced in November." Similarly, in his interview with William Attwood, published in the June 25, 1957, issue of *Look* magazine, Nasser said that in none of his speeches had he ever called for the destruction of Israel.

Unfortunately, however, just as Israeli nationalists proclaim their intention to expand "from the Nile to the Euphrates," so, too, Nasser makes fiery speeches, in the fashion of a cheerleader shouting to his football team, "Rip 'em and tear 'em up!" And even if Nasser himself has never actually called for the destruction of Israel, the Egyptian press and the inflammatory Cairo "Voice of the Arabs" broadcasts certainly have frequently done so.

The fact we have got to reckon with is that in the Middle East climate of fear, suspicion, hatred and exacerbated nationalism engendered by the tragic cycle of injustice, violence, retaliation and counter-retaliation, it is now practically impossible for the leaders on either side to pursue a policy of moderation leading toward reconciliation and peace. In order to retain the support and leadership of their peoples, they are compelled at the very least to make belligerent speeches. Even Nuri Pasha of Iraq said during the Suez War that all the Jews in Palestine should be sent back whence they came. King Husein of Jordan hastened to proclaim his uncompromising hostility to Israel after breaking with Egypt. And our friend King Saud is not only anti-Israel, but refuses to permit any Jews, even Americans, to enter his kingdom.

On the Israeli side it is equally difficult for any political leader to be temperate and rational and express a desire for compromise and reconciliation by means of even a token compensation for the losses sustained by the Arabs at Israel's hands. Israel's fears for her existence are not only real but also better founded than Arab dread of her as the "spearhead of Western imperialism." She is only a small island of less than two million people in the midst of the Arab sea and the Islamic ocean. Surrounded as she is by enemies, her survival is due more to the courage, dedication, endurance and hard work of her people than to Western financial and political support. In the conditions of hardship and danger in which most of her people live, a militant morale is necessary to sustain her. Unjust to the Arabs as was the partition of Palestine to make way for the establishment of a Jewish state, Israel has earned her right to exist. We would be committing yet another injustice in the cycle were we to let Arab extremists acquire the means to destroy her. Nor can we demand that Israel abandon her strategy of defense by attack unless she can win security by other means. But since true security for her is possible only on condition that she accept definite boundaries and abandon her aim to ingather the Jews from everywhere in the world, she must accept her status as one among many Middle Eastern states. The plain fact is that, without American financial and political support, Israel cannot live without the Arabs, and must learn how to live with them. In a word, freedom and justice for Israel depends on freedom and justice for the Arabs. This gives us our opportunity to produce a just and viable peace. Indeed it places on us the duty and responsibility of doing so.

Reason and material self-interest, unfortunately, play a small role in international affairs as against national ambitions, passions, prejudice and fear. Were this not so it would be easy to convince both the Israelis and Arabs that they have far more to gain through reconciliation and cooperation than by continuing to expand their energies in seeking to conquer or destroy one another.

Israel could supply the knowledge and skills, acquired in Europe by her immigrant citizens, to help the Arabs in Palestine and Jordan to catch up on the technological progress of the West, if she would abandon her ambition to expand and dominate, and if the Arabs could be induced to forgive and forget the injuries they have suffered at her hands. The Israelis and the Arabs together could make the desert bloom and supply a livelihood for both peoples, if they could be brought to cooperate in utilizing the waters of the Jordan River to their mutual advantage instead of letting them go to waste. The Israelis, if they would, might still be able to play the role of present-day Americans in raising the standard of life of economically backward peoples, instead of that of American pioneers who liquidated the Red Indians with no more compunction than the Israelis shoot up the Arabs who try to reoccupy the lands taken from them.

There are grounds for hope in the contrast between the attitude, character and aspirations of the "Sabras," meaning Jews born in Israel, and the old Zionists who still head the nation. According to the reports of a number of dispassionate Jewish and Gentile visitors to Israel, the Sabras repudiate or ignore Zionist visions, are "impatient" of Jewish traits and fealties, and wish above all to be able, constructive, self-contained, realistic and pragmatic, instead of pursuing Messianic visions based on the Torah or Talmud. They would seem, like the majority of the world's Jews, to be normal people who want to work in security and to develop their country, if only fanatic Arabs and fanatic Zionists will let them.

As Max Ascoli writes, the Sabras are inclined to "debunk a lot of old dogmas or slogans, including the "Ingathering of the Exiles." For a very large number of people, particularly young people, this same sympathetic, but objective, Jewish observer reports, "religion plays a rather limited role—or no role at all."

These "stolid, unintellectual, un-neurotic" Sabras, he continues, quoting a young Israeli officer, "will perhaps turn out to be a breed of men a bit closer to the Gentiles."

Dr. Theodore Huebner of New York University and Dr. Carl Hermann Voss, Lecturer at the New School for Social Research and Chairman of the Executive Council, American Christian Palestine Committee, reach a similar conclusion in their book called *This Is Israel* (New York Philosophical Library: 1956).

They say that there are young, intelligent Sabras who tend to repudiate the idea of the Diaspora, "the ingathering of the Jews," and their implications of "Jewishness," and who want to develop "a new national identity" which will include "a wider geographic and ethnic area free from the ideals of Zionism." Significantly, these Sabras are known as "the Canaanites," the name of the original inhabitants of Palestine. "Most of the younger Israelis," Huebner and Voss continue, "are opposed to the orthodox Judaism "which has been imposed on the nation" and believe that "the ethnic-religious basis of Israel is the chief obstacle to the complete realization of Western democracy."

Similarly, Waldo Frank, in his book entitled *The Drama of Israel,* reports that the rising generation regard themselves not as Jews, but as Israelis who repudiate or ignore Zionist Messianic pretensions, are impatient concerning "Jewish traits and fealties," and want only to win the right to develop their own State.

This all leads to the conclusion that ultimately Israel will abandon its attempt to establish a theocracy for all Jews, and become instead a normal secular State. Since many of its immigrants are Middle Eastern peoples more akin to Arabs than to Europeans, and because the generation born in Israel is apparently sick and tired of the Zionist myths and Messianic pretensions of their elders, it is entirely possible that the new State will eventually abandon its enemy-making policies and thus make it possible for her to come to terms with the Arab world around by becoming an integral part of the Middle East. As Professor Hocking of Harvard has expressed it:

> The first step toward sanity would seem to be a confession by Israel that the ideal of a national home, expressing the soul of the Jewish people is not realisable under human conditions; that the use of force and corrupt pressures

> must be discontinued, and that the flag of a religious fundamentalism alien to the present spirit of Israel will no longer be used to cover a crude political realism. I am not expecting this confession to be forthcoming, but its definition may work, in the silent places of men's thought where, after all, the forces of history are made.

Pessimists may say that it is already too late for America to exert her political, moral and economic influence to bring an end to the tragic conflict between the Israelis and the Arabs. Nevertheless there are grounds for hope that the prophets of disaster are mistaken. As John C. Campbell, a former member of the State Department's Policy Planning Staff, writes in the July 1957 issue of *Foreign Affairs*:

> Israel wants, above all, national security, which has just been proved unobtainable by her own efforts. . . . The Arabs want, above all, a more just settlement in Palestine. . . . Here is at least the opportunity to devise proposals that might satisfy the basic drives on both sides, even if immediate claims cannot be satisfied.

If we are to take advantage of the opportunity to satisfy the "Basic drives for security on both sides," we must first admit the validity of Arab grievances.

As all of us know in our personal relationships, individuals will forgive an injury if it is admitted and regrets are expressed, even when no material compensation is offered; but we also know that no amount of damages awarded by any court to the plaintiff can ever compensate for the refusal of the accused to admit that he was wrong. So also, if the Arabs are ever to be brought to make peace with Israel, we must first recognize their grievances and admit the justice of their case. If we acknowledged, and expressed our regrets at the injustice done to the Arabs and gave them valid assurances that they would not be required to make any further sacrifices, it might be possible to persuade them to accept Israel—if not within her present extended borders, in an area larger than that originally allocated to her by the United Nations. To bring this about it would be necessary for the United States to guarantee the future security of both Arabs and Israelis, and it would also be necessary for Israel to make some compensation to the Arabs she has dispossessed. Then the Arabs might well be induced to bury the hatchet, make peace with Israel, and allow her ships to pass freely through the Suez Canal and the Gulf of Aqaba.

An appeal to the Arabs' generosity for concessions for the sake of world peace might be far more successful than the attempt to coerce or intimidate them. Nothing, however, can be accomplished unless we try to understand the reasons for their intransigeance, cease giving our sympathy to only one side in the Israeli–Arab conflict, and give the Arab world reason to trust us again.

The situation is not hopeless, thanks to President Eisenhower's courageous and principled stand against the Anglo-French-Israeli attack on Egypt, and to the confidence in America which his speaking-out engendered among millions of Arabs. In the words of the most respected and best informed of British publications, the *Economist*:

> President Eisenhower electrified Asia and has won a respect he never previously enjoyed first by speaking without thought of the Jewish vote in the United States on the eve of a Presidential election, and then by the firmness with which he warned both his Anglo-French friends and Israel that they must conform to the will of the United Nations.

If President Eisenhower is of the stuff of which great American presidents are made, and if he is supported by the American people, he will be able to formulate and enforce a just and lasting peace between Israel and the Arab world, based on the principles which have made the United States great, strong, free and respected.

VI

THE CHALLENGE OF BOTH IMPERIALISMS

IN A GREAT SPEECH TO CONGRESS on July 2, 1957, Senator John F. Kennedy said that the most powerful single force in the world today is neither Communism nor Capitalism, nor the H-Bomb, but man's "eternal desire to be free and independent." The junior senator from Massachusetts may be over-optimistic, in view of the free world's desire for peace at almost any price, but he was eminently right when he said:

> The great enemy of that tremendous force of freedom is called, for want of a more precise term, imperialism—and today that means *Soviet imperialism* and, whether we like it or not, and though they are not to be equated, *Western imperialism.*

Some see only the challenge and menace of Soviet imperialism and would have us do nothing to help the peoples of Asia and Africa struggling to be free or independent, lest we injure the imperial interests of our French and British allies. Others would have us seek peaceful coexistence with the Soviet Empire and imagine that the specter of Communism can be laid by good works, meaning abundant economic aid to "underprivileged" peoples. John Kennedy is one of the few concerned with our failure "to meet the challenge of imperialism *on both counts* and thus failing in our responsibilities to the free world." He prefaced his speech, dealing at length with the Algerian problem which we have neglected, or refused to recognize as our problem, by saying:

> *Thus the single most important test of American foreign policy today is how we meet the challenge of imperialism,* what we do to further man's desire to be free. On this test more than any other, this nation shall be critically judged by the uncommitted millions in Asia and Africa, and anxiously watched by the still hopeful lovers of freedom behind the Iron Curtain. If we fail to meet the challenge of either Soviet or Western imperialism, then no amount of foreign aid, no aggrandizement of armaments, no new pacts or doctrines or high-level conferences can prevent further setbacks to our course and our security.

In contrast to Senator Kennedy, many Democratic and Republican opponents of Eisenhower's stand on Suez argued that, since we could not, or dared not, take any action to stop Soviet Russia's bloody suppression of the Hungarian Revolution, we should not have insisted that Israel, Britain and France withdraw from Egyptian territory. By some strange logic which can be understood only by acceptance of the premise that two wrongs make a right, some eminent conservative senators and columnists who on other issues could always be counted upon to take a principled stand, argued (as did Henry Hazlett in the *National Review* of February 9, 1957) that Israel should not be compelled to obey the United Nations by evacuating the Gaza Strip unless there was also "an immediate withdrawal of Russian troops from Hungary and from every other satellite nation where they are not wanted."

Thus, once again, as when Palestine was partitioned, it was

considered just and proper by many Americans that the Arabs should be called upon to pay the penalty for Europe and America's sins of commission or omission. In 1947, when Truman and Stalin jointly pressured the United Nations to establish the State of Israel at the expense of the inhabitants of Palestine, the argument which won approval for this act of injustice against the Arabs was the need to make restitution to the Jews for their abominable treatment by Nazi Germany, and to provide a home for the Jewish victims of persecution whom we ourselves refused to admit to our lands. Ten years later a majority in Congress, including even Senators Knowland and Bridges, who supported the administration's stand on the Suez War, were in effect saying that because we dared not risk war with Soviet imperialism by effectively supporting the Hungarian fighters for freedom, the Arabs must again be penalized, lest it be said that Israel was punished for her aggression while Soviet Russia went unscathed. Fortunately, President Eisenhower, as he himself said on February 20, 1957, did not believe that two wrongs make a right. Undeterred by the clamor in Congress and the press, Secretary of State Dulles backed the United Nations in its successful endeavor to force or persuade Israel to withdraw from the Gaza Strip and from Sharm el-Sheikh on the Gulf of Aqaba.

In my interview with Nasser, when I brought up the subject of Hungary, he did not pretend, like Pandit Nehru, that Russia was not imperialist, or condone her oppression of the Hungarians. Instead he said that the Anglo-French attack on Egypt had been an attempt to subjugate a free country, whereas Russia's action in Hungray was comparable to France's in Algeria: both were seeking to retain possession of a colony by suppressing a native rebellion.

Such distinctions are unimportant in comparison with the undeniable fact that the West's case against the Soviet Empire is immeasurably weakened by such acts of imperialist aggression as the Anglo-French-Israel attack on Egypt, and by France's suppression of the Algerian Liberation movement.

Whether or not it is true, as has been alleged, that the bombing of Egypt encouraged Moscow to go all out in her bloody suppression of the Hungarian revolt, it is certainly true that it diverted the attention of the "uncommitted" countries of Asia and Africa and thus caused far less damage to the Communist cause among the neutrals than would otherwise have been the case.

We feel much more deeply the wrongs and sufferings of members of our own family than we do those inflicted on our neighbors. Just as we Americans, because of our kinship with Europeans, were much more outraged over the crushing of the Hungarian Revolution than we were over the invasion of Egypt, so contrariwise in Asian and African eyes the invasion of Egypt was far more alarming and brought far greater condemnation than Russia's re-occupation of Hungary. And to ties of kinship of blood and culture was added the force of kinship of experience, since in Africa and Asia the Suez War revived fears of the reestablishment of British or French colonial rule. Even the Sudan and Iraq, which had no love for Egypt, rallied to her support because, as Dr. Ibrahim Anis, the Sudanese Ambassador to Washington, said to me later, "We feared that if Britain reconquered Egypt, we would suffer the same fate."

By intervening on Egypt's side against England, France and Israel, Soviet Russia was enabled to redeem herself in African and Asian eyes, or at least to cover up her own far bloodier and more ruthless aggression against Hungray. Thus it has been said that England and France helped Moscow to suppress the Hungarian Revolution by their attack on Egypt. This is, no doubt, an exaggeration since, given their fear, and America's, of a war with Russia, nothing would probably have been done to restrain the Kremlin even had there been no Suez War. That war is finished, and its consequences to the West rendered far less harmful than they would have been had America not taken her stand on principle and thus to a large extent redeemed "the West" in Arab eyes.

We are, however, still faced with the Algerian problem, which, like Israel, has now become our problem, and one concerning which we can no longer afford to behave like Pontius Pilate. In the case of Algeria, as in that of Israel, we shall neither retain nor win friends or exert influence if we continue to shirk our responsibility.

France enjoys a unique position in America. We excuse her when we would condemn others. We continue to regard her as the fount of liberty and the cultural center of the West, although she no longer has any valid claim to these distinctions. While we treat England as a wife whom we may disagree with and even chastise while remaining sure of the unbreakable bond between us, we treat France more like a beloved mistress to whom everything must be forgiven, because we fear losing her or because we dread her tantrums. Thus the American record concerning French imperialism is worse than it is with respect to British or Israeli imperialism. We have exerted pressure on Britain on various occasions to hasten her relinquishment of imperial privileges or powers; and although we have financially supported Israel, we have also restrained her, and we have refused her arms to match those being supplied to Egypt by Russia. But we have done nothing, except occasionally make a feeble verbal plea, to induce France to come to terms with the Algerian Liberation movement instead of continuing her futile, bloody and costly endeavor to suppress it. Worst of all, we have acquiesced in her utilization in Algeria of NATO divisions together with the American weapons, planes and other equipment intended for the defense of Europe, thus making ourselves a party to the suppression of the Algerian resistance.

Being thus involved, it is as immoral and hypocritical as it is dangerous for us to continue pretending that the bloody struggle in Algeria is an "internal" French problem which does not concern us or the United Nations. In Senator Kennedy's words:

> The war in Algeria, engaging more than 400,000 French soldiers, has stripped the continental forces of NATO to the bone. It has dimmed Western hopes for a European common market, and seriously compromised the liberalizing reforms of OEEC, by causing France to impose new import restrictions under a war-time economy. It has repeatedly been appealed for discussion to the United Nations, where our equivocal remarks and opposition to its consideration have damaged our leadership and prestige in that body. It has undermined our relations with Tunisia and Morocco, who naturally have a sense of common cause with the aims of Algerian leaders, and who have felt proper grievance that our economic and military base settlements have heretofore required clearance with a French government now taking economic reprisal for their assistance to Algerian nationalism.
>
> It has diluted the effective strength of the Eisenhower Doctrine for the Middle East, and our foreign aid and information programs. It has endangered the continuation of some of our most strategic air bases, and threatened our geographical advantages over the Communist orbit. It has affected our standing in the eyes of the free world, our leadership in the fight to keep that world free, our prestige, and our security. It has furnished powerful ammunition to the anti-Western propagandists throughout Asia and the Middle East—and will be the most troublesome item facing the October conference in Accra of the free nations of Africa, who hope, by easing the transition to independence of other African colonies, to seek common paths by which that great continent can remain aligned with the West.

France's claim that Algeria is an "integral part" of France is nonsense based on fiction. Its Moslem inhabitants, who outnumber the French settlers eight to one, have never been treated as French citizens, nor have any but a small minority desired to become Frenchmen. This, of course, is hard for the French to understand, since, in their conceit, they imagine that there can be no higher goal. Educated Algerians, like Tunisians, Moroccans and many Egyptians, having studied in French schools and universities, appreciate French culture as much or more than American Francophiles. This cultural affinity was France's trump card, but she discarded it by her failure in North Africa to apply any of the three great principles of the French Revolution: Liberty, Equality and Fraternity. Moreover, very few of France's colonial subjects get any education at all.

The plain fact is that Algeria is a colony, ruled over and held down by nineteenth-century methods which are unworkable once a subject people acquires national consciousness and a thirst for liberty and has the courage and cohesion to fight for freedom and independence. The irony of the situation lies in the fact that France, which finds it difficult to govern itself, claims the right to govern others, clings to her overseas empire without the economic strength or military power and prestige to maintain it, and claims Great Power status while depending on American subsidies to keep her own economy going and to equip the armed forces she employs to suppress the rebellion of those she holds in subjection. Her attempt failed in Indo-China in spite of the billion dollars directly or indirectly contributed by America. There she lost all, gave the Communists their chance to acquire part of her former territory, and—as I learnt in Saigon in September 1956—left a legacy of hatred or contempt for France. She relinquinshed her hold on Morocco and Tunisia at the eleventh hour, saving something from the wreckage. But instead of preserving and developing such friendly sentiments and cultural and economic ties as remained, she is now alienating both countries by her behavior in Algeria

—and by the rebuffs she has administered to the Sultan of Morocco and President Bourguiba of Tunisia, whenever these pro-Western Arab statesmen have endeavored to bring peace through negotiation and compromise between the Algeria nationalists and France.

The Moroccans and Tunisians, besides their fellow feeling for those still under the French yoke, fear the consequences to themselves should American arms enable France to crush the Algerian Liberation forces. They have reason to believe that General Juin was speaking for France when he said: "We must win in Algeria. If we triumphed in Algeria, we could then reconsider what we gave to Tunisia and Morocco. If we did not, we should lose what we still have in those countries."

This statement, published in the Paris paper *Le Monde* in May, 1957, was, of course, broadcast by the Cairo "Voice of the Arabs" with telling effect as proof that "French imperialism still harbors malice toward Tunisia and Morocco."

In sum, by her Algerian policy, or rather by her reliance on brute force in place of a policy—as also on account of her not only having sent jet planes to Israel but also French pilots to help her fly them in her war against Egypt—France has united the Arab world against her.

Even Iraq helps the Algerian Liberation Army. This I learned at a Washington reception, when a member of the Iraqui Embassy, defending his country in an argument with a girl refugee from Palestine, claimed that his country had materially helped the Algerians.

This incident is one among many I could relate to show the solidarity of the Arab world on both the Algerian and the Israeli issues. It has been revealing to observe at cocktail parties at the embassies of many of the Islamic countries, the cordial and friendly relations between their representatives, even at times when Egypt and Syria were supposed to have been "isolated" from Jordan, Saudi Arabia and Iraq. Nor is the underlying solidarity—or, at least, recognition of a common interest and identity—confined to the Arab countries. I learned this, thanks to having been in India, Pakistan and Iran in November 1956, as also on account of a personal experience in America the following spring. The *New York Times* had published a letter of mine giving the "other side" in the Suez Canal controversy, and I had also written an article in *National Review* called "Dissent on Egypt," which was widely distributed by the American Council on Islamic Affairs. Either by letter or by personal expressions of appreciation in Washington, I received thanks from representatives of Afghanistan, Pakistan, Iran, Iraq, Jordan, the Sudan, and Tunisia, as well as Syria and Egypt.

As in the case of Egypt, sympathy for the Algerians is not confined to the Arab world, but extends to all countries in Asia which were formerly subject to Western imperialism. In the words of the Pakistan Ambassador to the United States, Syed Ahjad Ali, in a speech to the American Friends of the Middle East in 1955:

> The keynote to the international relations of the modern nationalistic states of the Middle East is nationalistic agitation against any type of foreign control. . . . Even after the emergence of independent governments in recent years, Western powers, especially Britain and France, retained considerable economic and military privileges. North Africa is still struggling for elementary political rights. Unless these can be achieved the forces of nationalism are bound to find their main expression in anti-imperialist agitation [instead of internal development.]

The Eisenhower Doctrine will avail us little if we take no account of this basic fact. Having enlarged our world responsibilities to include the Middle East, we can no longer afford to sit on the sidelines while France continues to undermine the free world politically, morally and militarily by her war against the people of Algeria. For that in fact is what it is. The Algerian Liberation forces, according to the testimony of the very few English and American correspondents who have had the opportunity to observe them, are a national army. For instance, Donald Beichman, after spending three days and nights with the rebels in their secret command posts across the Tunisian border, reported in the July 29, 1957, issue of *Newsweek*: "It is difficult to call it anything but an army. From what I saw, it has discipline, manpower, weapons, command, and spirit. It is not a rabble."

An Englishman, Peter Thornycroft, gave the same testimony in pictures, when N.B.C. showed the film which recorded his much longer sojourn with the Algerian Liberation army. The showing of this film was preceded by Mr. Thornycroft's statement that he admitted being prejudiced against the French because they had knocked out several of his teeth and broken both of his wrists—thus subjecting him to the same treatment many Algerians have suffered at French hands. French brutality has incited the Algerians in their turn to mass murder of innocent people by placing time bombs in public places and to assassination of individual Frenchmen and their Moslem collaborators. As in Palestine, a cycle of injustice, retaliation and counter-retaliation has become faster and more furious, each evil deed producing more and more outrages committed by both sides.

Prejudiced or not, Mr. Thornycroft's film, showing the Liberation army in training and action, the victims of French bombing and burning of villages, and the Algerian nurses tending the wounded in hidden retreats, constitutes irrefutable testimony that the French are up against a resistance movement more formidable than was their own during the years of German occupation.

Some Frenchmen distinguished by their moral courage have pointed up the parallel. For instance, in April, 1957, M. Jacques Peyrega, Dean of the Algiers Law School, made public a letter he had written to the Minister of National Defense, Bourges-Manoury, in which, after describing outrages and crimes he had himself witnessed, he wrote as follows:

> When one is on the scene, when one hears all these rumors, when one has examples of their probable truth, one is seized with horror, one tells oneself that the Germans, under the Nazi regime, also did not want to know that they were being held responsible for horrors and that they too thought that it was only a case of a few abuses.

Similarly, T.T. Servan-Schreiber (a supporter of Mendes-France, who let Tunisia go free), in a book called *Lieutenant in Algeria,* has given an eyewitness account of French shooting of innocent Algerians. He recounts how when he protested he was told that scruples were suitable only for a Paris salon, and how the killings were "justified" on the assumption that every Arab is a potential rebel. This, of course, implies that the only way France can hold on to Algeria is by genocide.

A few other Frenchmen, Englishmen and Americans have described the Nazi-type methods of the French, including torture of prisoners by the *gonflage à l'eau* (forcible injection of water by a reverse stomach pump), and by the electric-shock belt-device perfected by the Gestapo. And by 1956 there were reported to be 40,000 Arabs interned in vast filthy concentration camps outside Algeria, according to Paul Johnson, assistant editor of the British labor-liberal *New Statesman,* in his book *The Suez War* (New York: 1957).

Whereas in England the Labor Party, which is generally anti-imperialist, condemned the attack on Egypt, in France where a Socialist government was in power at the time of the Suez War, Socialists cheered like everyone else. Similarly as regards Algeria, the myth that Algeria is a part of France has been staunchly upheld by the Socialists, who had no scruples in repressing the native rebellion with fire and sword. There is, however, some opposition, led by André Philip, who in a book called *Socialism Betrayed* calls the Port Said expedition a sin, and France's Algerian policy "a crime." And on the conservative side, a third book, also published in Paris in 1957, entitled *The Algerian Tragedy,* by the world renowned writer on the staff of *Figaro,* Raymond Aron, demonstrates that Algeria is not, and cannot be, an integral part of France and that "Algerian nationality" must be recognized, as much for economic and demographic reasons as because of the insurrection.

France's failure during the past three years to defeat the Liberation army, although her armed forces in Algeria must outnumber it by at least four to one, affords evidence of the strength of the Algerian Liberation movement. All her modern American equipment—including helicopters, which are the weapons most dreaded by the rebels—have not sufficed to crush the fierce and determined resistance of the Algerians, because, although they are ill-equipped in comparison with the French, they can rely on the greater part of the population for aid and support in their guerilla warfare. Month by month and year by year, France's brutal repression and her inability to protect her collaborators from reprisals inflicted by the underground, or by the army of Liberation, drives more and more Algerians into the ranks of the rebels. At the beginning of the revolt their numbers amounted to only a few thousand; by 1956-57 the Liberation army was estimated at around 100,000 men. Yet France goes on trying, at a cost of blood, treasure and reputation incalculably greater than any future material benefit she would secure, even if she succeeded in maintaining her colonial role in Algeria.

Lovers of France, who would have us continue to foster her illusion that she is still a Great Power by aiding and abetting her in her futile and brutal endeavor to keep the Algerians in subjection, are in reality doing her a great disservice. America would prove a better friend of France if we gave support to those Frenchmen who are sufficiently intelligent and courageous to face up to realities, who understand that France is ruining herself economically, as well as morally and politically, by her present course. We could, and should, shock France into facing realities by serving notice on her that she can no longer count on America for dollars, arms and political support in the United Nations whenever the Algerian issue is raised.

Hitherto we have done precisely the opposite. In 1955, when the United Nations Security Committee was asked to place the Algerian issue on the agenda of the National Assembly, the United States representative insisted that the matter could not properly be discussed because Algeria is an "integral part" of France. In 1956-57, when in spite of us the Assembly listened to the Arab States' appeal on behalf of the Algerians, Ambassador Lodge voted to postpone discussion for yet another year, and once again expressed firm faith in France's good intentions in Algeria.

Meanwhile Ambassador Dillon in Paris was as usual providing grist for the Communist propaganda mills. Inspired, no doubt, by his all-consuming love of France and desire to please her, he put America in the worst possible light in Asian and African eyes when he told a French audience that he "recalled with pride" that the "United States has consistently supported France when North African subjects have been discussed in the United Nations." After also calling attention to American military equipment made available for French use in Algeria, our former ambassador to France proclaimed that the United States "stands solemnly behind France in her search for a liberal and equitable solution of the problem in Algeria."

Just how "liberal" and "equitable" France's solution was, then as now, being amply demonstrated by military repression, the obliteration by American-made jet fighter-bombers of villages suspected of harboring or aiding the rebel forces; mass arrests and imprisonment of suspects, Gestapo-like methods of extracting confessions and administering collective punishment, and refusal to negotiate with the National Liberation front, unless and until the Algerian nationalists agreed beforehand to give up their struggle for freedom and independence.

In *El Maujahid,* the organ of the National Liberation front, issued in the French language by the publishing house called *Résistance Algérienne,* "the historic mission of the Algerian revolution" is stated to be "the final destruction of the odious and decadent colonial regime which is the obstacle to peace and progress."

The means by which the Algerians expect to win are stated to be: "total weakening" of the French army; the deterioration on a grand scale of the colonial economy by means of sabotage, rendering normal administration impossible; maximum disturbance of the French "economic and social system" in order to render continuance of the war impossible; and "the political isolation of France in Algeria and the world." Since the Algerians have demonstrated their determination to go on fighting—and have good cause to believe that if enough of them are ready to die for liberty, France will be unable, if only for financial reasons, to continue the war—France will, sooner or later, be compelled to let Algeria have her liberty. The longer she delays the more she is likely to lose, since the more bitter the war becomes, the less chance there is of a settlement which would save something for France from the wreckage.

The best that France can hope for is a settlement which would enable the million or more French in Algeria, while losing their master-race status, to retain their lands and live in security in an Arab State; but these "colons," who are responsible for the worst outrages against the Arabs, constitute the main obstacle to a settlement. France is underpopulated rather than overpopulated, and some of her fertile land is uncultivated or undercultivated. But, like Mussolini, who at the time of the Abyssinian War wanted the most unruly elements in Italy "to die as heroes or stay as colonists," France does not want *her* "colons" in Algeria to come home and make trouble. Their return is desired least of all by the Socialists who fear they would reinforce the reactionary "Right" or "Fascist" elements in France—which may be one reason why the Socialist government of M. Mollet appointed the diehard Robert Lacoste as Governor-General of Algeria and increased the number of French troops in Algeria from 250,000 to 400,000, when Lacoste claimed that this would enable him to crush the rebellion (which he has singularly failed to do).

Up to now the leaders of the Algerian rebellion have both held off from association with the Communists and abjured any intention of "throwing Algerians of European origin into the sea." Their struggle, they say, is neither a civil war nor a religious war. Their "war aims" are proclaimed in the following words, which I have translated from the French original version: "The Algerian Revolution aims at the conquest of national independence in order to establish a democratic and social republic guaranteeing real equality among all its citizens without discrimination."

History shows that the harder and longer the struggle for national liberation, the greater the power and influence acquired by extremists. Hence the stupidity of France in failing to come to terms with the Algerians before extremists get control of the Liberation movement. To quote Senator Kennedy once again:

> The fever chart of every successful revolution—including, of course, the French—reveals a rising temperature of terrorism and counter-terrorism; but this does not of itself

> invalidate the legitimate goals that fired the original revolution. Most political revolutions—including our own—have been buoyed by outside aid in men, weapons and ideas. Instead of abandoning African nationalism to the anti-Western agitators and Soviet agents who hope to capture its leadership, the United States, a product of political revolution, must redouble its efforts to earn the respect and friendship of nationalist leaders.

Another friend of France, Mr. David Schoenbrun, writes in his book, *As France Goes*:

> France must either gamble on the friendship of a free North Africa or get out of North Africa completely. It should be evident after the Egyptian fiasco that France cannot impose her will upon some 22 million Africans indefinitely. Sooner or later the French will have to recognize the existence of an Algerian state. The sooner, the cheaper in terms of money, men, and a chance to salvage something from the wreckage of the French Union.

France's hope that she will be able to recoup the huge financial loss she is incurring by her Algerian war through exploiting the oil riches of the Sahara will prove to be nothing but a mirage, unless and until she lets Algeria go free—simply because it is practically impossible to get the oil out through the rebel territory which separates the newly discovered oil fields from the Mediterranean.

If the French were the intelligent, enlightened and logically minded people they pride themselves on being, they would long since have recognized that their brutal game in Algeria is not worth the candle. And if the United States would, at long last, cease giving political support and financial and arms aid to France, she would be forced to realize the bankruptcy of her policy. Thus, we might at one and the same time save France and salvage our own reputation as the champion of freedom and self-determination of all peoples.

Perhaps nothing can bring France to reason and cause her to follow England's example in giving up colonies which are no longer profitable. If so, then we must regretfully decide to let France take her own road to perdition without us. For, even if Paris was worth a mass in the days of Henry of Navarre, today all France is not worth the alienation of the entire Arab world and the betrayal of our own faith in liberty.

France herself has helped to make all the Middle Eastern countries concern themselves with Algeria. For instance, George Weller reported from Damascus in a dispatch published in the *Chicago Daily News* on May 31, 1957, that when back in 1955 Syria sought to avoid accepting Czechoslovakia's long-standing offer to provide tanks and jet planes denied her by America and Britain, Syria as a last resort begged them from France. But as the Syrian Chief of Staff told Weller, "The first condition France made to selling us arms was that Radio Damascus and Radio Cairo must silence their broadcasts about Algeria. . . . We use Soviet arms," he continued, "only because the West has let us down."

I knew George Weller well in China during 1945-46, when he was one of the few American correspondents there who never fell for the Chinese Communist propaganda line. He is one of the most intelligent, perceptive correspondents I ever met, and he has always tried to tell the truth without fear or favor—hence the value of his dispatches from the Middle East, giving the Syrian side of the case. His account of the present situation on the Israeli-Syrian border, published on June 5, 1957, shows why the Syrian Government needs the arms denied her by the West. In a dispatch from Daughters of Jacob Bridge he wrote:

> On the strained Jordan River front where Syria confronts Israel, however, the U.N.'s peacemaking is in decline. For nearly 10 years U.N. border patrols have been steadily losing authority, mainly in Israel.

> U.N. morale is low. U.N. officers are discouraged, apathetic or even humiliated. . . .
>
> The piecemeal pressure wearing down the United Nations comes largely not from the ragged refugees but from dynamic Israel.
>
> Syria, weaker and less aggressive than Israel, has been a poor second in chipping away U.N. authority.
>
> In the words of one Scandinavian U.N. officer: "When Israel breaks the truce it is a mistake but when Syria infringes it is a crime. . . ."
>
> These . . . [armed forays] have left on both sides of the Jordan and the eastern side of Tiberias an array of bombed and bombarded villages, terrified and resentful Arab farmers and U.N. officers helplessly waving orders.
>
> Only a fraction of the United Nations' humiliation reaches the international public. Its setbacks are often suppressed by careerminded officers unwilling to commit their defeats to paper.

In the same dispatch Mr. Weller contrasts these "setbacks" on the Jordan River front with the success of "quick, courageous action by the U.N. and disciplined neutral troop movements" on the Suez-Gaza front, which "smoothed the way to peace."

Unhappily, as we have already observed, the fruits of the United Nations action on Suez, backed by the United States, are now in danger of withering on the vine. Russia, taking advantage of the little cold war we are waging against Egypt, is spreading the idea, easily accepted by Arabs, whose past experience renders them suspicious of the West, that the United States is seeking to step into Britain's vacated imperialist position, by keeping the Middle East divided and impotent. However, Nasser himself, to judge from his most recent speeches and interviews, is still giving America credit for our stand on Suez and still hoping for an entente with the United States and Britain to extricate him and his people from the Soviet embrace.

On the occasion of the fifth anniversary of the Egyptian revolution in July, immediately after the military parade displaying Soviet tanks and planes, the Egyptian president acknowledged that "we cannot deny America's attitude during the aggression and the condemnation of such aggression, as well as its attitudes in the United Nations." But naturally he also expressed his disappointment or "bitterness" at America's changed attitudes following the Suez War: "They plotted the starvation of the people. . . . America refused to sell wheat to us, intending to cause famine and so realize by peaceful means the objectives which France and Britain realized by war."

In the words of *Time* magazine, the tone of Nasser's speech was that of a "frustrated man with a grievance, but not that of a caged tiger." It suggested "that he knows as well as anyone else that the only way to end his country's economic stagnation and fear for the future is to get back on better terms with the West."

In an interview in Cairo in June with Basil L. Walters, Executive Editor of the Knight newspapers, Nasser showed that he understands Communist methods, and has greater political sagacity than those who have smeared him as a Communist stooge, or puppet, when he said:

> The only way to save the Middle East from Communism is by helping nationalism. If, instead, you push colonialism into a clash against nationalism these two will destroy each other. What will survive? Communism.
>
> The reason Communism is sure to win such a struggle is because Communist leaders are far better trained as underground organizers than nationalists. The Communists won the innocent nationalists into their control by playing on their patriotic sentiments.

It should be noted that Nasser and his "junta," in screening the lists of candidates for the Egyptian "Parliament" for whom the electorate might vote, struck off the names of known Communists, as well as of the other extremists, the Moslem Brotherhood, described by George Weller as a sort of Arab Ku Klux Klan.

Gamal Abdel Nasser is distinguished by his quick wit as well as by his charm which friends and enemies alike recognize, and which the latter regard as his secret weapon. Replying to Mr. Weller's query, "Are you a dictator?" he said:

> Dictator or liberator, it's how you look at it. Lincoln used to tell the fable of a shepherd who prevented a wolf from eating his sheep. To the sheep he was a liberator. But to the wolf he was a dictator.

In his account of this interview, published in the *Chicago Daily News* on June 17, 1957, Mr. Walters stated a truth ignored by others who think in stereotypes of a past era. "Dictator or liberator," Mr. Walters wrote, "Nasser does not fit into the usual pattern of either. Like so many young men of the Middle East, he is something brand new and old labels don't apply." Or perhaps Nasser is not brand new, but rather a representative in the Middle East today of the forces similar to those which made the nations of Europe in the eighteenth and nineteenth centuries.

The British authors of the Penguin Special entitled *Middle East Crisis,* to which I referred in an earlier chapter, describe Nasser as "the leader and symbol of those who wish to unify, or at least to lead, the Arab lands"; and they compare the Arab world today, divided into a number of soverign states, with Germany a hundred years ago:

> Among the intelligentsia is the conviction that the state of affairs is transitory, and that somehow Arabia should be unified, either by federation or by the triumph of one of the Arab countries over the others. As in Germany, the re-

sistance from the so-called particularist groups is strong. Unification would destroy many vested interests. But the aspiration to unify is genuine.

Nasser's enemies endeavoring to paint him in fascist and Nazi colors, have gone so far as to compare his short book, *The Philosophy of the Revolution,* with Hitler's *Mein Kampf.* No one who has read Nasser's book can accept this thesis. On the contrary, it shows that, far from being a fanatic nationalist, he is seeking for a way to ensure freedom, dignity and progress for his people, without any clear notion as to how it can be done.

In keeping with the fact that the Egyptians are traditionally the least Arab of the "Arabs," regarding themselves rather as heirs of the Pharaohs than as sons of the Prophet, Nasser's original ambition would seem to have been that of becoming a new Rameses (whose statues he is supposed to resemble) rather than a modern Caliph. In his own words, in an interview with Keith Wheeler published in *Life* magazine:

> Here we are ready to be Arabs, but also we have been Egyptian for 6,000 years, and why should we give that up? There have been many plans for Arab unity, but they all failed because they meant political union and the people suspected they really meant the leaders wanted to dominate. This is why I could not plan any domination even if I wanted to.

The forces of history were too strong for Nasser to become simply an Egyptian nationalist. As Guy Wint and Peter Calvocoressi write: "He is called upon from many sides to be the Bismarck of Arabia, and to unite his peoples from the Atlantic Ocean to the Persian Gulf."

In an oft-quoted passage of his book, Nasser himself writes:

> The pages of history are full of heroic and glorious roles which never found heroes to perform them. It seems to me

> that in the Arab circle there is a role wandering in search of a hero. This role, exhausted by its wanderings, has at last settled down, tired and weary, near the border of our country, and is beckoning to us to move, to take up its lines, to put on its costume, since no one else is qualified to play it.

Egypt resisted and stemmed the Mongol tide which ravaged the Arab world to the north and wiped out the flourishing civilization of the Euphrates and Tigris valley. Her universities and schools provide teachers all over the Arab world, and she has for centuries been recognized as its cultural center. Her geographical position makes her the link between the Arab world of Asia and that of North Africa. Her population of twenty-four million makes her the largest of the Arab states. Although Nasser may fail in his attempt to make her predominantly non-Arab population behave like Arab heroes, the leading role of Egypt in the Arab struggle for independence and strength through unity is not to be denied. As another perceptive British writer, the Right Honorable Anthony Nutting, who resigned his position as British Minister of State for Foreign Affairs in protest against the attack on Egypt, wrote in the May 12, 1957 issue of the *New York Herald Tribune:*

> Because the rulers of the inter-war years accepted the division of the Arab world, and their successors were too indolent or corrupt to try and change it, Nasser has become a popular hero whose picture adorns the bazaars from Marakesh to Bahrein. Not only does Nasser claim to have thrown off the yoke of those who divided Arabia, but many of the inarticulate masses see in him the promise of that unity without which they cannot treat on equal terms with the West and with Israel.

In sum, the only hopeful course for America and the free world to steer in the Middle East is, as John C. Campbell writes in the April 1957 issue of *Foreign Affairs,* "one which frankly accepts Arab aspirations for self-determination, equality and independence, but sets limits to support of extreme claims which deny these rights to others."

When I was in the Middle East last December, I saw the Arab peoples once more turn their faces toward the West, as Eisenhower's intervention in the Suez War reawakened the same hopes that had been raised by Woodrow Wilson's Fourteen Points almost forty years ago. Since my return, I have realized from the dispatches in the press that Arab enthusiasm for the United States was giving way to bewilderment, as succeeding American policy seemed to contradict our previous strong stand against the Anglo-French-Israeli aggression. Now I learn from Americans who visited the Middle East in the summer of 1957, and from Arab friends there who are friendly to America, that a reversal in the Arab attitude toward the United States is taking place.

Whereas the Eisenhower intervention in the Suez War was first regarded as an expression of traditional American devotion to freedom and justice, it is now increasingly regarded as a cynical time-serving action by which the United States hoped to make easy its inheritance of the imperialist role of Britain and France in the Middle East. The enunciation of the Eisenhower Doctrine; our dispatch of the Sixth Fleet to Western Mediterranean waters; our bolstering up of King Husein's government against the opposition of the majority of his people favoring Arab solidarity; our efforts to isolate Nasser and to force King Saud into opposition to him; our continued refusal to speak out against Israeli megalomaniac ambitions and for justice to the refugees she has dispossessed; our indirect bolstering of France in her crushing of the Algerian Liberation movement—all these, in Arab eyes, make the American action during the Suez Canal Crisis seem only a new method of achieving the old, familiar imperialist end. Once more, it appears to the

African and Asiatic peoples, the West is preparing both to betray its own ideals and to frustrate the legitimate aspirations of the "lesser breeds."

Thus the Arab-China parallel continues. My friends also report that, more and more, the Arabs are looking to Soviet Russia for support. They are careful to distinguish, I am told, between "Soviet Russia" and "Communism." It is not an ideology that they seek, but help to realize their own, non-Communist aspirations, which require arms to protect themselves against aggression and economic aid to develop the good life they desire. So, tragically, the Arabs, like the Chinese before them, repulsed by the West, may fall for the old illusion: that help from Russia does not mean submission to Communism.

If we in the United States wish to turn the tide back in our favor, and to save the Middle East from the Communist threat, we too must rid ourselves of a long-standing illusion: the illusion that America and Europe are one and the same. True, the United States is part of the West, and many of our traditions and devotions are the same as those of Europe. But America is much more than Europe transplanted overseas. In essence, the United States afforded Europe the opportunity to make a new beginning in new surroundings, where the richness of an unused continent presented the hope that Western man could purge himself and his institutions of wrongs and injustices that had corrupted the European ideal.

When, in the course of history, the men transplanted from the old continent to the new raised a banner inscribed with the words "that all men are created equal, that they are endowed by their Creator with certain unalienable Rights," they no longer called themselves Europeans, but Americans.

It is not America's role to turn back to Europe—to identify herself with the old ways from which we fled. America's role is not to support the decadence of Europe, but to recall her to her better self; not to bolster up the privileges and perquisites of dying principalities and powers, but to speak for liberty, justice, and decent living for individual men.

It was with this hope that the first settlers turned their eyes West; and it has been for these things that many people, including myself, have followed them in later years. If the United States will reassert with pride her devotion to the ideals that have made her great—and formulate these ideals, as she can if she will, in terms of practical policy—then the peoples of the Middle East, along with all the others in the world who desire so greatly the things that Americans both represent and enjoy, will also turn West. For then they will know that to turn West means not subjugation, but Freedom.

BIBLIOGRAPHY

BIBLIOGRAPHY

Antonius, George. *The Arab Awakening.* London: Hamish Hamilton, 1955

Atiyah, Edward. *The Arabs.* Penguin

Beal, John Robinson. *John Foster Dulles.* New York: Harper, 1957

Beatty, Ilene. *Arab and Jew in the Land of Canaan.* Chicago: Regnery, 1957

Berger, Elmer. *Who Knows Better Should Say So.* New York: The Bookmailer, 1956

Bromberger, Merry et Serge. *Les Secrets de l'éxpédition d'Egypte.* (Editions des 4 Fils) Paris: Aymon, 1957

Cheng, Tien-fong. *A History of Sino-Russian Relations.* Washington: Public Affairs Press, 1957

Egypt, Republic of. *White Paper on the Nationalisation of the Suez Maritime Canal Company.* Cairo: 1956

Foot, Michael and Jones, Mervyn. *Guilty Men, 1957.* New York: Rinehart, 1957

Guillaume, A. *Islam.* Penguin

Hoskins, Halford L. *The Middle East.* Macmillan, 1954

Hudson, G. F. *The Far East in World Politics.* London: Oxford Press, 1937

Huebener, Theodore and Voss, Carl Hermann. *This Is Israel.* New York: Philosophical Library, 1956

Hutchison, Commander E. H., U.S.N.R. *Violent Truce.* New York: Devin-Adair, 1956

Isaacs, Harold. *The Tragedy of the Chinese Revolution.* London: Secker and Warburg, 1938

Will the Middle East Go West?

Izzeddin, Nejla. *The Arab World.* Chicago: Regnery, 1953
Johnson, Paul. *The Suez War.* New York: Greenberg, 1957
Lengyel, Emil. *Egypt's Role in World Affairs.* Public Affairs Press, 1957
Lilienthal, Alfred. *There Goes the Middle East.* New York: Devin-Adair, 1957
Lilienthal, Alfred. *What Price Israel?* Chicago: Regnery, 1953
Nasser, Gamal abdel. *The Philosophy of the Revolution.* Cairo: "Mondiale" Press
Shwadran, Benjamin. *The Middle East, Oil and the Great Powers.* New York: Praeger, 1955
Sparrow, Gerald. *The Sphinx Awakes.* London: Robert Hale, 1956
Tang, Peter S. H. *Communist China Today.* New York: Praeger, 1957
Teller, Judd L. *The Kremlin, the Jews and the Middle East.* London and New York: Yosel, 1957
Wint, Guy and Calvocoressi, Peter. *Middle East Crisis.* Penguin Special, 1957